MW01659767

Shift: Leading In Transition has real world applications for business leaders today.

— LUCAS INGALA, FOUNDER AND CEO, *WATCHMEN SECURITY*

This book is smart, poignant, and full of interesting and inspiring stories. I loved it!

— BRENT RUDOSKI, LEAD PASTOR, *FAITH ALIVE FAMILY CHURCH*

A leadership tune-up—that's what this book offered me! I was challenged by the principles that J.D. King brought forth in *Shift*. I discovered insights I need right now to navigate the organizations I lead. Frankly, there are all kinds of books on leadership, but this primer offers fresh wisdom for the biggest need of the hour—solid, godly leaders who can bring sustainable change to the world around them.

— BRAD HERMAN, PUBLISHER, *HARRISON HOUSE*

Knowing how to shift and pivot when necessary is one of the keys for long term success for any business or ministry. J.D. does a fantastic job in this book talking about the process and mindset needed to do just that.

— JUSTIN RIZZO, SONGWRITER AND WORSHIP LEADER, *INTERNATIONAL HOUSE OF PRAYER*

One thing that I've learned after years of studying leaders and the foundational principles of success, is that . . . shift happens. Another fundamental truth that I've come to realize is that leaders must adapt or die. In *Shift*, J. D. King does an incredible job of illustrating what adaptation looks like, using practical and innovative examples every aspiring leader can put into practice.

— PAUL KOPECKY, ENTREPRENEUR AND BUSINESS COACH, *KOPECKY BUSINESS GROUP*

The world is changing fast. *Shift: Leading in Transition* is exactly what we need. It's good to know that there are timeless principles based on the Word of God available for leaders today.

— DAVID WHITED, EXECUTIVE DIRECTOR, *SHOP.COM* AND FOUNDER OF *FLYOVER CONSERVATIVES*

What we need is a *Shift* from our natural way of seeing and thinking to God's divine wisdom. This easily accessible book offers many rich scriptural, contemporary, and historical insights that I believe you will find applicable and relevant.

— WILL RIDDLE, VICE PRESIDENT OF CHURCH PROGRAMS, *PRISON FELLOWSHIP*

J.D. King does a masterful job defining leadership essentials. His practical insights are what we need to cut through the clutter and advance beyond the uncertainties. Whether you're leading a business, church, or merely guiding your family, *Shift* provides the tools to navigate the transitions.

— JAMES KOPPANG, PASTOR, *WORLD REVIVAL CHURCH*

Focusing on both the *being* and *doing* of leadership, *Shift* moves past the fluff and gets straight to the point. In a world of social media influencers and fake online mentors, society needs to punch the reset button on what true leadership really means.

— DAVID PARK, ENTREPRENEUR AND LEADERSHIP CONSULTANT, *PARK GLOBAL*

Headed into a new era, we're on the threshold of a major shift. This book is for leaders who refuse to go back.

— DICK DRUMELLER, PASTOR, *CRYSTALBROOK CHURCH*

SHIFT

LEADING IN TRANSITION

J.D. KING

Christos

“Anyone can hold the helm when the sea is calm."

— PUBLILIUS SYRUS (85-43 B.C.)

Shift: Leading in Transition
Copyright © 2021 by J. D. King

Christos Publishing
Post Office Box 1333
Lees Summit, MO 64063

First Printing, in the United States, April 2021.
For Worldwide Distribution
All rights reserved.

ISBN 978-1-950053-19-3

For other exciting releases from Christos Publishing visit our store:
www.TheResurgenceStore.com

Cover design by Shawn Jonas | sjonas@wrckc.com
Editing by Lisa Thompson | writebylisa@gmail.com

While all stories in this book are true, some identifying information has been changed to ensure privacy.

No part of this book may be reproduced in any form or by any electronic or mechanical means, including information storage and retrieval systems, without written permission from the author, except for the use of brief quotations in a book review.

Scripture quotations marked (NLT) are taken from the *Holy Bible, New Living Translation*, copyright © 1996, 2004, 2007, 2013, 2015 by Tyndale House Foundation. Used by permission of Tyndale House Publishers, Inc., Carol Stream, Illinois 60188. All rights reserved.

Scripture quotations marked (NIV) are taken from the *Holy Bible, New International Version*®, NIV®. Copyright © 1973, 1978, 1984, 2011 by Biblica, Inc.™ Used by permission of Zondervan. All rights reserved worldwide.

Scripture taken from the *New King James Version* (NKJV) ®. Copyright © 1982 by Thomas Nelson. Used by permission. All rights reserved.

Scripture quotations marked TPT are from *The Passion Translation*®. Copyright © 2017, 2018 by Passion & Fire Ministries, Inc. Used by permission. All rights reserved.

The Holy Bible, English Standard Version® (ESV®), Copyright © 2001 by Crossway, a publishing ministry of Good News Publishers. All rights reserved.

Holman Christian Standard Bible® Copyright© 2017 by Holman Bible Publishers.Christian Standard Bible® and HCSB® are federally registered trademarks of Holman Bible Publishers. Used by permission.

J. B. Phillips, "The New Testament in Modern English," 1962 edition, published by HarperCollins. All rights reserved.

Scripture taken from the *Holy Bible: International Standard Version* (ISV) ®. Copyright © 1996-forever by The ISV Foundation. All rights reserved. Used by permission.

Christos Publishing produces superbly researched Christian books informed by a Spirit-led worldview.

"We have different gifts, according to the grace given us. If a man's gift is ... leadership, let him govern diligently."

— ROMANS 12:6, 8

ACKNOWLEDGMENTS

I owe an enormous debt of gratitude to those who gave me freedom to test insight-related ideas in leadership seminars and consulting engagements over two decades. These conversations shaped the content of this book in a myriad of ways.

I'm also thankful for generous colleagues and friends who provided constructive comments. These individuals include: Esther Tsai, Tim O'Brien, Will Riddle, Kerre Story, David Park, Aaron Lage, and Phyllis DeMeo.

I'm likewise grateful for Pastors Steve and Kathy Gray and the leadership team at World Revival Church. What a sublime pleasure it is to work with individuals who want to change the world.

Finally, I want to thank my wife, Bobbie, for tolerating my incessant writing. A lifelong companion makes both the journey and destination worthwhile.

CONTENTS

INTRODUCTION

As I reached for the door, I spotted a smudged, handwritten sign: “Sorry friends, our store is closed.” A beloved local bookstore had gone out of business. As I discussed my disappointment with a colleague, he remarked, “Don’t be upset, J. D. It’s merely a sign of the times.”

Our society is transitioning, and not everyone likes the changes. Many have told me that the disruptions make them feel as if the ground is crumbling beneath them. While revolutions inaugurate innovations, they also subvert beloved institutions and practices.[1]

Of late, the reverberations have felt particularly intense. Life was relatively tranquil in the beginning of 2020, but two-and-a-half months later, the bottom fell out. George Galloway, a Scottish Parliamentarian, aptly remarked, “Nothing can happen for decades, and then decades can happen in weeks.”[2]

Part of what we’re contending with is the metamorphosis of long-held structures. Whenever the media changes, society changes too. Celebrated communication theorist, Marshall McLuhan, said it like this: “We become what we behold. We shape our tools and then our tools shape us.”[3]

As we glance backwards, the evolution from oral to print culture in the fifteenth century disrupted Europe—sparking the Reformation, scientific inquiry, and the Industrial Revolution. Unexpectedly, the linear arrangement of books reconfigured other elements, even in churches. Shane Hipps observes,

> The linear arrangement of pews in churches didn't exist before the printing press. The medieval church didn't have pews—just a wide-open space for standing. After the printing press, church seating started to mirror the page of a book.[4]

In the twenty-first century, a different revolution is occurring. For better or worse, the internet is rewiring civilization although some cringe when they hear this. But humanity's sense of identity, reason, and function are being reconfigured. Whatever forms our stories tends to shape our world.

CRISIS ACCELERATES

Many incremental modifications have been instituted since the dawning of the twenty-first century. The reordering of relationships (and physical space) through our phones and digital tools was gradual—until now.

In 2020, a health crisis hastened changes that would have normally taken a decade or more. I'm talking about the COVID-19 pandemic.

Families were facing a mysterious virus that *The New York Times* nicknamed "The spiky blob seen around the world."[5] As it traversed the continents, it jeopardized billions of lives. Some disruptions are impossible to ignore.

Some are convinced that the coronavirus outbreak is "the hinge event of modern history, a moment that forever alters its course."[6] This prognosis is probably overblown, but the pandemic is, nevertheless, accelerating disruptive technology.

During the COVID-19 quarantine, businesses rapidly went remote. Transactions through digital channels increased, jumping from 16 percent of purchases to higher than 27 percent.[7] Companies began emphasizing contactless payment options. Business meetings "went virtual, every teacher became an online educator, and social gatherings moved to a screen."[8] This crisis also launched a "tsunami of innovation around remote medicine and tele-health."[9]

A myriad of digital innovations that transformed society was instituted in a matter of weeks. But the tremors were also being felt in numerous other realms.

SOCIAL CHANGE

For multitudes, the technological disruptions were less abrasive than the social and political changes. But don't be mistaken; they are merely different aspects of the same unfolding reality. When the major structures change, the underlying societal cracks begin to show. The disruptions didn't cause them; they just exposed them.

Older Americans were shocked as social justice advocates protested during the lockdown. The tragic death of George Floyd, an impoverished Black laborer, enraged millions. Derek Chauvin, a White Minneapolis police officer, turned him upside down, handcuffed him, and knelt on his neck. During this fracas, Floyd repeatedly asserted, "I can't breathe." Many believed that Floyd's death by asphyxiation on May 25, 2020, was an emblem of institutional racism.[10]

Because of Floyd's death, a protest movement called Black Lives Matter recruited millions of White supporters and people of color online. With branded signs, hashtags, and memes, they took to the streets, marching against injustices in a digital and public rebuke.

Antifa, a left-wing, anti-fascist, and anti-racist movement, also arose during the aftershocks of this tragedy. They exploited violent tactics, looting, burning, and tearing down monuments, all in an effort to achieve their goals. As musician Gil Scott-Heron quipped, "The revolution will not be televised."[11]

Within the insurrectionist milieu, the "digital generation," Millennials (1981–1996) and Gen Z (1997–present), developed a "stewing sense of class resentment."[12] Assertive White moms were mockingly called "Karens."[13] They also ridiculed their affluent "elders" with the retort, "Okay, Boomer."[14] By exploiting the hashtag #EatTheRich, they reasserted the radical wisecrack, "When the people shall have nothing more to eat, they will eat the rich."[15]

Within this wrangling, political animosities intensified. Before the pandemic, America was already experiencing "pronounced polarization."[16] The religious, economic, and social fissures separating urban and rural interests verged on eruption for years.

Conflicts between red and blue states (and individuals) appeared unsurmountable. Some claimed that foreign powers were compromising digital voting machines in swing states. Others accused White nationalists of acts of insurrection organized through Twitter, Parler, and other social media apps. Technology is supposed to unite us but often divides us. Few can find common ground in a society torn asunder.

Mask mandates, social distancing, censorship, and forced lockdowns had a catastrophic impact. With a myriad of disruptions, the global marketplace was in flux. The May 6, 2020, edition of *The New York Times* reported that the American unemployment rate had reached 14.7 percent—the highest level since the Great Depression.[17]

Many unsettling events were taking place, but what has been most troubling is the spiritual fragmentation. Churches are trying to connect with people online but struggling to do so. Because of the turmoil, thousands of churches were closing down. Church analyst Tony Morgan said, "1 out of 5 churches will close over the next 18 months . . . 25% of North American churches are vulnerable. That is over 60,000 Protestant churches."[18]

Throughout neighborhoods, individuals are losing their sense of wonder as they struggle to survive. Anxiety has grown so widespread that there aren't enough counselors to help.

Many view establishment voices with suspicion. An embittered colleague told me, "You can never trust these fat cats in Washington. They are up to no good." Others believe that our societal structures are unsustainable—maybe even a hinderance. Do traditional American institutions—health care, jobs, schools, courts, churches, government, and law enforcement—require radical restructuring? Who gets to decide?

A segment of our society wants to tear everything down and start over. They see this ensuing calamity as an opportunity for a "Great Reset."[19] They maintain, in this era, there's a chance to end inequalities and make things right.

Others want to eradicate the "Deep State"—an entrenched network of government bureaucrats reportedly entangled in corruption. Wherever one stands, both idealism and conspiratorial fears are rampant in America.

With all the infighting and saber rattling, reverberations echo. Jerry Lee Lewis, the rock-n-roll icon, used to sing a song called, "Whole Lotta Shaking Going On."[20] This is an apt refrain in the midst of the aftershocks. A friend from Minneapolis messaged me, saying, "What else in my neighborhood is going to collapse? We've already lost so much."

In the Bible, the writer of Hebrews said that things would be "shaken and removed, so that only unshakable things will remain" (Hebrews 12:27 NLT). What else will be unhinged in the ensuing revolution? The answer still awaits.

HISTORY REPEATS ITSELF—OR DOES IT?

Defining present-day matters is complicated. You probably already know this, but these issues can easily be mischaracterized. All of us are prone to oversimplify, seeing situations differently than they are. Over the years, so many have stumbled into this trap.

It's imperative to take a look at the big picture as we examine our predicament. We are not the only ones who have struggled with adversity. History shows the prevalence of technological changes, plagues, and upended cities. In the preceding centuries, catastrophes frequently occurred.

The Bubonic Plague, or the Black Death, decimated Europe from 1347 to 1351. As this disease spread from Rome to London, bodies suffered from black boils that oozed blood and pus. The horrific symptoms included: "fever, chills, vomiting, diarrhea, terrible aches and pains—and then, in short order, death."[21] This dreadful pandemic slaughtered one-third of Europe.

Civilization splintered in the aftermath of inexplicable death. Monarchies and long-standing economies collapsed. With so many peasants dead, the land laid idle. Due to the scarcity of labor, the nobles had less bargaining power. In successive decades, the stranglehold of feudalism lessened.

Scorned in the fallout from the Bubonic Plague, the poor "questioned entrenched hierarchies." Their resistance enabled Europe to "break out of its medieval malaise." These developments set into motion "the Renaissance, Reformation, and Enlightenment. From death and horror came science, modernity, and growth."[22]

This virus upended centuries of medieval culture, opening the door to modern society. In a myriad of ways, civilization was reconfigured in the aftermath of the Black Death.

Not every pandemic has the same impact on society. My mom recently informed me that my grandfather, Seldon Day, contracted the Spanish Flu as he returned from fighting in World War I.

Apparently, agonizing symptoms attacked his body: nausea, fever, and diarrhea as a bloody, frothy fluid filled his lungs. Fortunately, he recovered, but many of his countrymen didn't.

From 1918 to 1920, the Spanish Flu killed 50 million—when the global population was only 1.8 billon. Government officials urged city dwellers to don cloth masks and social distance. The 1918–1919 health campaigns elicited the same kinds of controversies and squabbles that we witnessed in 2020.

What's surprising is that this pandemic had no long-term impact. When comparing the fallout from the Spanish Flu to the Bubonic Plague, one would expect similar patterns. But this was not so. Newspapers and other archival sources indicate little change. Rather than looking backward, Americans eagerly hailed the Jazz Age and the Roaring Twenties.

Journalist Fareed Zakaria, in his examination of that era, made the following notes:

> There is little evidence that people worked differently or socialized less after that gruesome outbreak. There was no new normal, just normal . . . People went back to their farms, factories, and offices because there was no alternative. To work, you had to be at work. If you sought entertainment, you would find it only in theaters and music halls. If you wanted to buy food or clothing, you needed to go to a brick-and-mortar store.[23]

One would expect a monstrous disease to reshape the national psyche and spark a myriad of disruptive changes. After all, that's what occurred in Europe centuries before. But the catastrophe that should have changed everything, altered nothing. Our ancestors were mostly indifferent.

Maybe the ravages of World War I had already hardened our families, and as Zakaria suggested, they had no alternatives. But it's astounding that this pandemic barely left a mark on their life stories. I never knew that my grandfather had the Spanish Flu until 2020. It wasn't a notable part of family lore until now.

CRAVING SOMETHING DEEPER

As we try to find our way in the third decade of the twenty-first century, it's difficult to know how far the digital and societal disruptions will go. Will America encounter the kinds of upheaval fourteenth-century Europeans faced, or will our experiences be more akin to the era that produced the Spanish Flu?

Who are we, and where do we stand? The future may depend on the stories that we hear and the individuals who tell them to us. This may or may not change everything.

Neither futurists nor historians possess what's needed to push us forward. The masses require something more. Individuals, amid an existential crisis, crave something other worldly. Both the young and the old are aching for something uncommon in our culture—compassionate strength. I'm convinced that authentic leadership, rooted in the love of God, can cut to the heart of all our dilemmas. This is the key to finding the way forward.

Some will embrace a life-giving posture and make a positive difference. They will see beyond themselves and serve the needs of multitudes.

Amid the disruptions are extraordinary opportunities. Spirit-led innovators, compelled by grace, can shift culture. Entrepreneurs, educators, politicians, and ministers can't shrink back. They must reinstitute the foundations of leadership and implement them in every sphere of responsibility.

A PRACTICAL GUIDE

This book—*Shift: Leading in Transition*—is an attempt to assist with the most formidable need of the hour. It's a practical guide for navigators to circumvent a rapidly changing world.

In the succeeding pages, I investigate the meaning and sphere of leadership. Drawing upon history, Scripture, and practical examples, I revisit foundations and functional strategies for reestablishing compassionate authority in the twenty-first century.

Some of what I scribble on these pages will sound familiar. There's something enthralling about the "mystic chords of memory."[24] An experienced older preacher used to tell me about the power of remembering. He said, "As you're reminded of what you already know, transformation occurs." Old voices can carry us forward.

Don't let well-trodden truths pass from your consciousness too hastily. Solutions might be rooted in something you already know. Discoveries have a cyclical quality. T. S. Eliot the beloved poet, said that the "end of our exploring" is to "arrive where we started and know the place for the first time."[25]

Hopefully, not everything in these pages will be old hat. This book will surely break some fresh ground here and there. Different pathways provoke unanticipated questions. Interruptions can be a seedbed for innovation. The great sage, Solomon, reasoned, "It is the glory of God to conceal things, but the glory of kings to search them out" (Proverbs 25:2 ESV).

Extraordinary men and women will boldly advance into the chaos, engaging questions without immediate answers. In fact, the eagerness to ascertain truth is a definitive sign of a leader. How you see and engage says a lot about you.

Those with nobility and strength will eagerly forge new trails, anticipating what lies over the horizon. They know that exploration can open the door to revelation.

I want to invite you on a journey of discovery. In establishing your path, you may help myriads of others discover their destinies as well. It's time for a renewed understanding of leadership. Collectively, we can navigate difficult transitions and redefine an entire generation. It's time to shift culture and revolutionize the world.

—J. D. King
Kansas City, Missouri

1

LEADING WITH A WEAK HAND

"Why didn't you follow up? Robert's upset that no one checked on him. Now he refuses to take anyone's calls. Weren't you close to him and his family? What happened?"

I was at a loss for words. No one wants to have this kind of conversation with their boss. In situations like this, the weight of a mistake can feel overwhelming.

I apologized and assured my supervisor I'd work to make things right. But sadly, I couldn't fix the problem. An untreated wound will invariably worsen with time. I wept as one I'd invested several years in was gone from my life.

Most of our problems arise from faulty assumptions and wrong decisions. Beneath our dilemmas, we often face the aftermath of leadership failure.

I hate it when problems arise and detest it even more when I'm the cause. I don't think I considered the potential of problems until I trudged through some of my own struggles. I couldn't deny these issues when I saw them face-to-face.

I have made mistakes that caused me to question whether I could be a competent leader. These mishaps also brought internal issues to a head. This is a hard truth, but trouble seldom comes into focus until it's personal.

To make our way forward, each of us must grapple with underlying problems and renegotiate the rigors of leadership. This, in many ways, is the fundamental aim of this book.

Whether leading in a crisis or in other contexts, we have to find our way forward.

WEAK LEADERS

Changes sometimes come through unexpected means. I knew an older businessman that I occasionally met with. Jim was generous with his time and wisdom. I marveled at the way he took simple truths to a deeper level. This gifted man shared much insight.

In one of our meetups, Jim spoke with me about various leadership problems. No one was better at illustrating truth through storytelling than he was. I loved hearing from him.

In this conversation, Jim brought up Asa, a Judaean monarch in the Bible. He explained to me, "Understanding concepts is easier when we have concrete examples. Seeing is understanding."

Jim said, "Asa was a 'good man' who failed. Most people think that a noble man can do no wrong, but that's not so. All kinds of great people mess up. That was true in the ancient world, and it's true today."

Continuing, he explained, "Before we talk about Asa's mistakes, we need to make it clear where he stood before the Lord." Jim then turned to one of the Bible passages that summarized Asa's life: "Asa did what was right in the eyes of the Lord, as his father David had done . . . Asa's heart was fully committed to the Lord all his life" (1 Kings 15:11, 14 NIV).

Jim explained that although Asa desired the things of God, weaknesses undermined his leadership. My friend mentioned three areas of concern: 1) Asa failed to remove the destructive items. 2)

Asa initiated improper relationships. 3) Asa refused to trust in the power of God.

1. FAILURE TO REMOVE THE DESTRUCTIVE THINGS

This business owner clarified that a leader has to be willing to purge. Sometimes responsible parties need to remove more than they add. Leadership can be as much about subtraction as addition. I had never heard that notion before.

Jim emphasized, in this particular situation, God commissioned Asa to take down the idols and wicked things in Israel. This Judean king made progress, even removing the evil artifacts from his own home. Yet, Asa was unwilling to go all the way.

> King Asa even deposed his grandmother . . . because she had made an obscene Asherah pole. He cut down her obscene pole, broke it up, and burned it in the Kidron Valley. Although the pagan shrines were not removed from Israel, Asa's heart remained completely faithful throughout his life. (2 Chronicles 15:16-17 NLT).

Asa's love for the Lord was never in question. Nevertheless, his noble intentions didn't result in appropriate actions. When push came to shove, the monarch wasn't willing to go the distance.

Asa allowed a mixture of good and evil to muddy the waters. He didn't make the distinctions between God and the false idols as clear as they should have been. This confusion likely blocked spiritual renewal. Negligence can hinder the blessings of God.

Sometimes clearing the slate opens the door to growth and development. Leaders should remove everything that keeps people from finding their destiny.

2. AN IMPROPER RELATIONSHIP

Jim pointed out another event that happened during Asa's stint of leadership—an inappropriate covenantal relationship. He reiterated that our intimate associations matter. We generally become whoever we're aligned with. As the saying goes, "A man is known for the company that he keeps."

Early in Asa's reign, Ethiopia tried to overtake Judah, but God stepped in and stopped the invasion. Later, as the nation of Aram was maneuvering toward them, the Lord intervened once more.

However, Asa made a grave error. In the Ethiopian crisis, Asa turned to God first, and the situation worked out. But in the second conflict, he acted without consulting the Lord, taking a shortcut and making a blood covenant with Aram. Judah became like a "brother" to this wicked nation. The Bible narrates the following:

> Asa removed the silver and gold from the treasuries of the Temple of the Lord and the royal palace. He sent it to King Ben-hadad of Aram . . . along with this message: "Let there be a treaty between you and me like the one between your father and my father". . . Ben-hadad agreed to King Asa's request . . . Hanani the seer came to King Asa and told him, "Because you have put your trust in the king of Aram instead of in the Lord your God, you missed your chance to destroy the army of the king of Aram. Don't you remember what happened to the Ethiopians and Libyans and their vast army, with all of their chariots and charioteers? At that time, you relied on the Lord, and he handed them over to you. The eyes of the Lord search the whole earth in order to strengthen those whose hearts are fully committed to him. What a fool you have been! From now on you will be at war. (2 Chronicles 16:2–4, 7–9 NLT)

For short-term gains, Asa formed an intimate relationship with the wretched nation. This association undermined God's purposes.

Because of this dreadful decision, the nation of Aram remained a thorn in Judah's side for decades.

Wrong relationships wreck everything. So competent leaders are mindful about who they partner with. They would never covenant with the wrong individuals or institutions. Improper alignment destroys everything.

3. REFUSAL TO TRUST IN THE POWER OF GOD

Jim said Asa was a well-intentioned leader, but he kept running in the wrong direction. Whenever a leader gets in trouble, he or she has to know where to turn.

In an unexpected development, Asa became afflicted with a terminal sickness in the later years of his reign. Rather than resting on the strength of the Lord, he relied on "witch doctors." This was a disastrous choice.

> In the thirty-ninth year of his reign, Asa developed a disease in his feet, and his disease became increasingly severe. Yet even in his disease he didn't seek the LORD but only the physicians [witch doctors]. Asa died in the forty-first year of his reign and rested with his fathers. (2 Chronicles 16:12–13 HSCB)

Although Asa loved the Lord, he had only nominal faith in his regenerating power. This afflicted king should have sought God but, instead, embraced the short-sightedness of the masses. Leaders should rise above the fray, but Asa didn't.

God could raise Asa. All that the afflicted king needed to do was petition him. But Asa did not turn to the Lord or allow him to intervene in his most challenging moment.

During a crisis, Asa was prone to take the easy way out, resulting in ineffective leadership.

DON'T LET YOUR HANDS BE WEAK

Jim said that problems are usually evident beforehand in a leader's life. Like a myriad of others, Asa's shortcomings emerged at the beginning of his rule. To remedy this, the prophet Hanani was dispatched with the following message from God:

> "Listen to me, Asa . . . The Lord is with you when you are with him. If you seek him, he will be found by you, but if you forsake him, he will forsake you . . . Be strong and do not let your hands be weak." (2 Chronicles 15:2, 7 NIV)

Jim glanced my way and blurted, "Good intentions, or even a sincere desire for God, are not always enough. Leadership is not just about matters of the heart but also requires appropriate actions."

As I nodded, he said, "You must be good-hearted and possess a love for God, but you need much more. Leaders have to advance with Spirit-led purpose and strength."

As we wrapped up our lunch, Jim told me, "Asa's story teaches us that though good, a leader with weak hands can still be ineffective, resulting in problems. We must be strong where it matters."

In our many talks, Jim motivated me to confront shortcomings and grapple with vulnerabilities. What's striking is that he did most of this indirectly. The stories Jim told about others were really about me.

As I walked away that afternoon, I recognized that Jim addressed my struggles. Asa's story, in many ways, intersected with my own deficiencies. This seemingly random narrative was what I needed to begin some soul-searching. A change came out of that moment, for which I'm eternally grateful.

OVERHEARING STORIES

I'm not as good of a storyteller as Jim is, but I endeavor to follow his example. One of the most compelling ways to learn is to listen to the stories of others. Narratives engage us in inexplicable ways.

The issue at hand is leadership. This book is about how to navigate the waters of influence. It's tough to move beyond the periphery to get to the heart of matters. We often trip over our own obstacles.

Few regard themselves as "bad leaders." No one honestly thinks, "I'm the villain of the story." In their minds, it's always someone else's fault. I heard one misguided manager say, "I'm not mistaken. I'm misunderstood."

Reality is considerably more complicated than any of us realize. A chasm exists between *truth* and *perception*. You might not know it, but issues invariably lie beneath the surface.

Perhaps reflecting on failed leaders in various spheres can provide an opportunity for self-exploration. This permits us to see situations in a different light and grapple with some of our own shortcomings.

Many well-intentioned authorities sadly undermine their own directives. Their tragic lives remind us of the dangers of veering off course. It's easy to get entangled. So leaders sometimes need ugly stories to remind them of what actually matters.

WEAK LEADERS IN THE MARKETPLACE

I've had the privilege of working with a variety of marketplace leaders over the last two decades. I've met with directors of Christian organizations, authors, and real estate developers. Farmers, restaurant owners, and multi-level marketers have also sat at the table with me.

Since I own *Christos Publishing*, a small enterprise, I like to gain wisdom and a rundown of best practices. Occasionally, I'm on the receiving end of counsel, but other times, I'm the one sharing lessons. Either way, the conversations are valuable.

My colleagues and I desire to get ahead and figure out how to succeed in our labors. This isn't unusual. Anyone working to establish something wants it to grow.

In the business realm, just like any other, leadership is crucial. Governance without purpose will collapse. Individuals making a difference in their field tend to possess foresight and strength. They are transformational leaders.

Enterprise is expanding globally, but not all of it is rooted in competent models. Many businesses will not survive the coming years because of short-sighted leadership.

We can learn lessons from failed business leaders. Let me share a few stories with you.

BORDERS BOOKSTORES

In the early 2000s, the Borders bookstore chain was struggling. To offset some of their quarterly losses, the CEO increased their CD and DVD offerings. While other retail chains were scaling back, Borders vastly expanded their merchandise.

Borders had no strategy to capitalize on the burgeoning digital market. The board of directors didn't consider the impact of e-books. Their chief brick-and-mortar rival, Barnes & Noble, developed the Nook digital reader, but Borders had no similar plans.

To use a sports analogy, Borders took their eye off the ball at a critical moment in the game. The company's leadership team was extremely short-sighted, and it cost them greatly.

By 2011, Borders announced they were shutting down two hundred stores. Faced with liquidating $350 million of inventory, the company was stuck and just couldn't turn things around.

Because of inept decisions, Borders bookstores went bankrupt and were forced to close. The beleaguered company had a weak leadership structure that didn't help them navigate the turbulent upheavals of a changing marketplace.[1]

Those who cannot embrace the future will be left behind in the ravages of the past. Tomorrow belongs to those willing to look beyond the horizon.

GENERAL MOTORS

General Motors, the maker of Chevrolet, is another example of what happens when leaders don't adapt to shifting marketplaces. Customers' expectations were changing, but GM wanted to keep making cars like they built in 1985.

Since they were the leading manufacturer for decades, GM didn't feel the same pressure to innovate that other corporations felt. Stuck in "cruise control," they offered consumers mediocre designs, modest fuel efficiencies, and insignificant upgrades.

Frequently, those on top believe they'll always remain there. GM was still selling a lot of cars at this time, and as the saying goes, "Never fool with a winning strategy." The retirement-minded board members didn't want to derail the gravy train.

However, by maintaining a stagnant approach, General Motors eventually fell from 50 percent to less than 20 percent of the market share. In 2009, Toyota ended GM's seventy-seven-year reign as the world's largest automaker.[2]

The *New York Times* observed, "GM towered over its competitors as the world's biggest automaker for more than 70 years," but now it is a more "middle-of-the-pack company in terms of sales and revenue." Shockingly, even as "GM racked up huge losses in recent years, the company hardly touched its bloated management ranks."[3]

The automaker's leadership team was so incompetent that in

2009, the US government had to infuse $50 billion in federal loans to save the company from bankruptcy.[4] While competitors like Elon Musk's Tesla continue to rise, General Motors continues to lag. The numbers don't lie. In 2020, Tesla was up 242 percent while GM dropped 31 percent.[5]

I'm all for baseball, hotdogs, apple pie, and Chevrolet,[6] but the future is not necessarily built on the past. Even in times of plenty, leaders must be mindful about what's ahead. Victory often comes to those who are proactive.

EASTMAN KODAK

A generation ago, the Eastman Kodak Company was arguably one of the most respected and profitable enterprises in the United States. The corporation made hundreds of millions of dollars by marketing film and photo paper. Nevertheless, this once-lucrative company tripped up in the late 90s, and the bottom fell out.

Like other businesses, the digital revolution caught Kodak ill-prepared. The CEO and teams were so preoccupied with film that they didn't consider different market segments. Kodak did not foresee the broad adoption of digital photography.

What's paradoxical is that the original digital camera was designed by a Kodak employee in 1975. He and other engineers experimented with digital imaging but missed key developments.

At the time, digital images didn't match the quality of film, so Kodak assumed consumers wouldn't be interested. They were wrong. Customers wanted immediacy and ease of use; quality was a secondary concern.

Digital technology continued to advance, but Kodak still dragged their feet. Although the corporation acquired Ofoto, a forward-thinking photo site, they hoped to market prints, not facilitate online sharing.

Although Western society was in the midst of a digital

revolution, Kodak insisted on remaining in the paper and film business. Scott D. Anthony, of *Harvard Business Review*, observed the following:

> There was a bitter war inside Kodak between the digital division and the print establishment. The top executives were fixated on getting people to print their digital photos. The digital division said people didn't care.[7]

Despite Kodak's efforts, families moved away from printing photos. Instead, they shared images on Facebook and other social media apps. Kodak didn't seem to understand that the quality of photo paper didn't matter to a digitally minded customer. They weren't looking to make artifacts; they wanted to connect and share life events.

Kodak leadership was so caught up in expanding their print sales that they didn't recognize the opportunities in online sharing. They struggled to see that "the digital economy was becoming so powerful that it was dominating—eating up—the material economy."[8]

This globally recognized corporation missed several cues and fell behind. After a century of innovation, Kodak went into bankruptcy in 2012. One of the most beloved companies of the twentieth century was no more.

Kodak was the best in the world at placing images on film and paper. But the industry changed. Their business models depended on the maintenance of a waning medium. Organizations have to lean into what the market demands, not what they prefer. This is particularly true during times of economic upheaval.

UNDERMINING THE ECONOMY

Once thriving businesses are collapsing. Magazines, newspapers, and the music industry were already in freefall a decade ago. But more recently, restaurants, theaters, music venues, and retail shops faced financial ruin.[9]

But long before the coronavirus pandemic disrupted marketplaces, business leaders were already tripping up.

JCPenny, Sears, and ToysRUs—retailers reluctant to launch digital stores—were either on life-support or bankrupt.[10] Leadership teams assumed families were more interested in coming into brick-and-mortar stores than in shopping online. They were wrong. As Scott Galloway, business professor at New York University, said, there's a "disconnect—between the big and the small, the innovative and the old-fashioned."[11] These discontinuities are more obvious than ever.

Businesses have been creeping in the wrong direction for a while. Stockholders and investors are livid. As many as 15 percent of CEOs in the United States might be fired in a fiscal year.[12] More recently, over 1,300 company heads were fired or resigned.[13] One can only imagine the aftermath of 2020–2021. Fareed Zakaria, a journalist and political commentator, uttered the following prediction:

> As COVID-19 accelerates the trend of digital retail overtaking real-life retail, over the next five years, by one estimate, around 100,000 brick-and-mortar stores in the United States will close—three times the number shuttered during the recession of 2007–9.[14]

Technological shifts are clearly upending established business models, and global economies are in transition. Digital encroachments, changing demographics, and COVID-19 regulations have sidelined operations.

But these underlying issues are not just rooted in health concerns, social unrest, or changing markets. Enterprises are failing because of inept leadership.

Businesspeople must lead with wisdom and purpose. In the midst of so many uncertainties, people long for decisive action. Authorities tied to Wall Street, the banking industry, and retail stores can no longer manage with a weak hand.

WEAK LEADERS IN POLITICS

In the 1970s and 80s, I grew up in the household of a politician. While Bill Clinton was still the governor of Arkansas, my father served as a State Representative. Let me tell you, I've witnessed first-hand the foolishness and ineffectiveness of government officials.

Elected officeholders are supposed to protect our freedoms and extend the constructive elements of society. Through their efforts, safety and prosperity should permeate our communities. But that is rarely what comes to pass.

Smiling politicians promise everything but deliver very little. Voters are hoping for visionaries but end up with bureaucrats with cheap theatrics and empty rhetoric. It would be funny if it weren't so tragic.

I have no desire to be a partisan. Both sides of the aisle often make their fair share of leadership mistakes. It doesn't matter whether Democrats or Republicans are leading Congress; very little gets accomplished. Sadly, effective leadership in the government sphere is quite rare.

History shows us endless examples of failed political leaders. Neville Chamberlain, the prime minister of England, comes to mind. He signed a "peace treaty" with Hitler, enabling Germany to stock up and prepare for the second world war. Chamberlain's accommodation of the Nazis ultimately brought turmoil and death to his homeland.

In a more recent example, President Hugo Chávez brought Venezuela into ruin. In this formerly prosperous nation, citizens are now starving due to his socialist policies. Chávez's political schemes failed the very people that he was called to serve.

Ineffective government leaders destroy the peace and prosperity of a nation. They often fail the people when they're needed the most. For centuries, society has been constrained by inept politicians. Voting records prove that people rarely learn lessons from history.

GENERAL GEORGE MCCLELLAN

Across the generations, politicians and war efforts have been entangled. Military figures loomed large in the arena of governance. One unsettling example is Abraham Lincoln's commander during the rise of the Civil War.

Although a capable strategist, building the army of 70,000 soldiers, General George McClellan was reluctant to attack. Shockingly, he "refused to move all through the year, despite mounting pressure from the press and Lincoln."[15] McClellan's lack of follow-through almost cost the Union the war.

After the general faced losses in subsequent battles, he blamed everyone but himself. Astonishingly, he even suggested that President Lincoln was the underlying problem. Every time that McClellan faced another crushing defeat, he refused to take responsibility.

As the conflict intensified, McClellan griped about not having enough soldiers or weapons. He even grumbled about the amount of pay that his infantry received. Leaders rarely have adequate resources, but effective ones get the job done anyway. Complaining never helps.

The general found ways to bypass direct orders and often defied the President. McClellan imagined that he was craftier than Lincoln and had plenty of excuses to justify his insubordination. Most of the President's inner circle could see exactly what was happening.

Lincoln gave McClellan numerous opportunities to correct his behavior and redeem himself. But in the end, he refused to change. He left Lincoln with no choice but to relieve the general of his duties.[16]

Poor leadership impacts a nation at war. It also undermines other spheres of authority. Bloodshed increases when politicians don't govern effectively.

PRESIDENT RICHARD M. NIXON

The idea of political failure brings to mind an event that occurred just before I was born—the fall of Richard Milhous Nixon. This politician's missteps tarnished the office of the President of the United States for a generation.

Although relatively popular with the electorate during his 1972 campaign against George McGovern, Nixon made some disastrous decisions that marred his legacy.

A covert team operating out of the White House basement attempted to bug the telephones of the Democratic National Committee, headquartered at the Watergate Hotel in Washington D. C.

This off-the-books team bungled the Watergate break-in and was arrested. Nixon wanted to make the scandal disappear and used the State Department to impede FBI investigations. Political espionage can be treacherous. But as terrible as Nixon's actions were, what undermined him was the cover-up.

After the break-in came to light, Nixon's robust economic policies and foreign diplomacy no longer mattered. He lied to the American people and betrayed their trust. There was no coming back from that disastrous decision. Nixon resigned in disgrace in 1974.[17]

Lies irreparably tarnish the prestige of an elected office. Political leaders should be held to a higher standard. There can be no more deception among twenty-first century leaders. Honor must be restored in this hour.

PRESIDENT JIMMY CARTER

Baptist Sunday school teacher and former Georgia governor, Jimmy Carter, was elected as president in 1976. The American electorate hoped that he would help put the Nixon scandal behind them.

Carter was hardworking and conscientious but was out of his element. Brimming with good intentions but low on know-how, he was a woefully ineffective leader.

During Carter's administration, Americans suffered from a severe economic downturn. The soaring unemployment, tepid monetary gains, and 18 percent inflation were paralyzing.

On top of this, a stifling, Middle-Eastern energy crisis hit American motorists. Waiting to fill their tanks, families lined up for miles at gas stations. The prices for fuel and other necessities skyrocketed.

As Carter presented ill-designed policies, Democrat and Republican members of Congress chastised him. He was so caught up in the minutia that he missed the big picture. He couldn't see the forest for the trees.

Carter's passion was "for how things are done, rather than what should be done." He placed "greater emphasis on methods, procedures, and instruments for making policy than on the content of policy itself."[18]

As matters came to a head, Carter wore a cardigan in a news broadcast, warning that the energy shortage might be permanent. To reduce consumption, he pleaded with families to turn down the thermostat and wear sweaters. Carter hoped to provoke action. Instead, he exasperated the electorate.

Although Jimmy Carter was a decent man, Americans did not want his incompetent leadership any longer. The Georgian was trounced in his re-election campaign in 1980. His challenger's television ad declared, "The time is now for strong leadership"[19]—an assertion that reminded voters of Carter's ineptitude.

This might seem counterintuitive, but good men might not govern effectively. Ethics matter, but it takes more than decency to lead a nation.

COVID-19 PANDEMIC

On January 23, 2020, the city of Wuhan, China, was partitioned off to stop the advance of a mysterious virus. Days later, the World Health Organization declared that this outbreak was a matter of international concern.[20]

By March, the novel coronavirus (COVID-19) was rapidly expanding, affecting the citizens of Italy, Saudi Arabia, Mongolia, and Qatar. It would soon be a global phenomenon.

In April, four billion people around the globe were in lockdown with all their movements and social engagements carefully scrutinized. This exertion of bureaucratic force had no precedent in modern history.[21]

While governments initially needed to furnish reasonable safeguards for the public, the ongoing regulations did not always make sense to the citizens.[22] It didn't help that in the U.S., 90,126 state and local governments devised "their own rules on mask-wearing and public gatherings."[23]

The conflicting guidelines and inconsistent policies frustrated many managers and owners. Private schools, restaurants, and churches were closed down. Because of the stifling mandates, some of these institutions never reopened.

Citizens were in the dark about what was mandatory. Local laws and conspiracy theories suddenly butted heads. As arguments erupted on social media, well-meaning organizations did not know how to mitigate the turmoil.

Journalist Fareed Zakaria pointed out the following:

> Though intended to save lives, the shutdown of nearly all activity led to economic collapse. This has caused untold hardship and ironically, exacerbated many health problems, from hunger to depression. Was it worth it?[24]

Murky leadership decisions disrupt society and make it difficult to overcome challenges. Governance during a crisis is not easy, but officials needed to provide *clear communication* and *definable benchmarks*. Cities needed politicians who could stand and provide solid action points. Sadly, the leadership often fell flat.

No matter how well-intentioned, authorities can't change the world by fiat. Arbitrary injunctions will never increase adherence or quell unrest. Leaders need to find transformative strategies to guide people in times of difficulty. Otherwise, society disintegrates.

LEADERS SET THE TONE

One of the reasons that the United States is divided is because of deficient leadership from our elected officials. The power brokers are often more interested in protecting their own interests than in bettering the lives of citizens.

Officials never seem to ask their constituents to peer beyond the horizon or dream of a better day. In fact, many bureaucrats hope that the people aren't paying attention at all. They've found that it's more advantageous to move along the periphery.

For the most part, citizens are in the dark. They don't know where we're going as a civilization. It's as if we're stumbling through the wilderness. The Bible reminds us, "Where there is no vision, the people cast off restraint" (Prov. 29:18 ESV). Without any meaning or purpose, individuals are prone to rebel.

For better or worse, those in seats of power set the tone for the citizenry. The magistrates establish and model everything a nation does. Within the contentious governmental sphere, it's time for visionary leadership. Society doesn't need more politicians with weak hands.

WEAK LEADERS IN THE CHURCH

Inadequate leadership is not only noticeable in the business and political sectors; it's also evident in the administration of Christian fellowships. Many analysts believe that the North American Church is in an existential crisis. Believers have somehow forgotten who they are and where they are going.

Over the last two decades, I've partnered with pastors, evangelists, and other local church leaders. I've had the privilege of visiting a myriad of congregations. I found some wonderful things in my journeys, but I also witnessed vexing concerns.

Although Christian congregations are expanding internationally, most are plateauing in North America and Europe.[25] In a majority of fellowships, money is tight, and participation is waning. On Sundays, more families are congregating at Starbucks or the soccer field than at church.

There's little doubt that "Western culture has shifted, and it has shifted largely against churches."[26] Colleges are forbidding Christian organizations from fraternizing on campus, and cities are exploiting eminent domain laws to replace churches with tax-producing stores.[27] Instead of being seen as the solution, Christians are blamed for duress. The favor that churches once received from municipalities is fading.

Evangelists and pastors have discussed their concerns with me.

Almost daily, I receive emails and phone calls, asking, "What's wrong?" A hostile political environment, health scares, and social duress are contributing to the marginalization of congregations. There's no doubt about that. But ineffective leaders are truly obstructing the gospel's advance. Myriads of ministry heads have lost sight of the originating mission.

Without structural changes and a fresh stirring from God, the Christian witness will be significantly diminished in the West. I don't find any joy in acknowledging this. God will have his way, but it might not be in our generation.

Even those who are not functioning in church leadership can benefit from some of the hard lessons disclosed here. Breakdown is unsettling, but increased sensitivity can help us keep our feet on the straight and narrow. Beauty is often hidden in the chaos.

THE ASSEMBLIES OF GOD

The Assemblies of God, a denomination that I grew up in, thrived for many decades. But in recent years, this Pentecostal fellowship has waned. Their story arc holds valuable leadership lessons.

In the beginning, the denomination's leaders focused on evangelism and ministering to the marginalized.[28] They directed their outreach efforts toward lower- and middle-income White families, which made up the bulk of the American populace at that time.

Yet as demographics changed, most Assemblies of God churches didn't pivot. While the leaders were busy extending their programs, an ethnic transformation was underway. Most local congregations went on as if everything were the same, but the ground was shifting under them.

Evangelical and Pentecostal church plants naturally cared "for those who lived in the community." However, over time, many churches "forgot their purpose." As the "neighborhood changed, the church did not change with it." Thom Rainer observes,

> Instead of adapting to a changing population, church members moved out of the neighborhood and drove miles to church. When the church membership demographic is significantly different from the community's, that church is already on a path toward decline.[29]

The Assemblies of God has plateaued, not only because of demographic shifts but also because of methodological changes. Evangelism and missions no longer held the same significance that they once did. Originating purposes are often forgotten as organizations age.

This is not just a problem within Assemblies of God congregations. Currently, only 2.2 percent of American churches are growing through conversions.[30] Thom Rainer's research team documented that 94 percent of evangelical churches are losing ground in their communities.[31] Many Protestant fellowships in America are stagnant or declining. All of this was before COVID-19 decimated everything.

Many are guardians, not innovators. Pentecostal and evangelical churches focus on maintenance, politics, and protectionism. The aging leaders are fighting to preserve a culture rather than expand the gospel. Very little growth comes from this outlook.

Darren Rogers, notes, in the *AG*, from 2001 to 2015, "the number of white adherents decreased by 1.6%, and the number of non-white adherents increased by 76.8%."[32] Some former members have withdrawn, and the remaining growth segments are primarily among minorities.

Assemblies of God congregations aren't the only ones struggling with cultural disruptions. Membership is also decreasing in Southern Baptist churches for similar reasons. Recent reports show that the SBC lost 2 percent of its membership. These losses reflected the biggest numerical drop in a century.[33] Congregational engagements not as it was.

Pastors can decry what has been lost, or they can regroup for another day. Many of the greatest leadership opportunities reside on the unexplored margins. Pioneers travel where few others go.

As we look ahead, leaders cannot disregard the evolving sensibilities of local communities. Immigrants and minorities will shape the destiny of twenty-first-century Christianity. Lorenzo Lebrija, director of TryTank Experimental Lab, observes

> In 2045, something amazing will happen in the United States. For the first time, the white population will dip below the 50 percent mark of the overall population. According to the Census Bureau, whites will make up 49.7 percent. Minority groups will outnumber whites in this country (Hispanics 24.6 percent, Blacks 13.1 percent, Asians 7.9 percent, and multiracial at 3.8 percent). In fact, by 2060 one in three U. S. residents will be Hispanic.[34]

If local churches don't adjust to this emerging reality, they'll be left behind. Tod Bolsinger argues that officials trained in outdated models "will never thrive as leaders as long as the majority-world voices around us are silenced."[35] Authorities cannot ignore the margins if they hope to move forward in the days ahead.

Stakeholders in established denominations must move out of a protectionist mindset. Leaders must adapt if they hope to maintain contemporary relevance. When the evangelists stop evangelizing, everyone suffers.

IT'S NOT ENOUGH TO SPEAK WELL

Situations can easily become misaligned. I don't want to chastise ministry leaders, but local pastors don't necessarily fare well in their leadership roles. There's a lot of confusion about what a church leader actually does. Ministry involves much more than preaching.

I knew a Midwestern charismatic pastor who lost the plot of the story. Michael was continually experimenting with how to bring congregational growth, but nothing materialized for him.

Michael was charming, and his sermons were well received. He had a lot going for him, but problems kept cropping up. I want to honor others, so I don't often listen to outside criticism. But this situation held genuine concerns.

The claims didn't shock me. These kinds of issues are not unusual. The Barna Group discovered that less than half of committed attendees believe their church performs its primary duties with excellence.[36] The Francis Schaeffer Institute of Church Leadership found that

- 62 percent of church members did not believe that their church leaders exemplified spiritual maturity.
- 68 percent believed that their pastors did not effectively disciple, motivate, or develop members for ministry.
- 74 percent felt that there was little to no equipping taking place.[37]

Dissatisfaction with a local minister is par for the course these days. American rebelliousness and independence run deep. Many, in the grassroots, dislike all authorities.

While criticisms are usually inflated, changes are, nevertheless, required. Leaders cannot ignore legitimate shortcomings because of ungracious criticism.

Michael always sounded energized when he spoke with me but didn't follow through in his local fellowship. He inspired but seldom resourced or mobilized. Despite significant needs, Michael rarely asked for contributions or volunteers.

I'm convinced that Michael loved God and desired the

kingdom's expansion. His intentions were decent, but he still led with a weak hand.

Leadership has to be more than noble intentions. There are lots of so-called good people no one is following. The congregants want more than just a nice guy. The masses are waiting for a leader who speaks, acts, and lays it all on the line.

Sadly, Michael never got the church off the ground and had to go back to his old insurance job. He may have been a strong preacher, but he was no leader. Lethargy and inaction cost him greatly. One simply cannot lead with a weak hand.

MARK DRISCOLL AND MARS HILL

When it comes to leadership in the local church, I want to point out another cautionary tale. Mark Driscoll was a new believer when he started Mars Hill Church in 1996. The twenty-six-year-old preacher was "dynamic and funny, with a potent mix of reverence for Jesus and irreverence for everything else."[38]

Driscoll's humor and blunt approach raised eyebrows. He, for example, mocked typical Christian portrayals of Jesus. Driscoll said that many churches were making the Son of God "an effeminate-looking dude" or a "neutered and limp-wristed Sky Fairy of pop culture."[39]

Driscoll's rhetoric and style were offensive, but that was part of the charm. Mars Hill's unconventional approach drew the alienated, tattooed, and pierced to Jesus, like few others. Their unconventional church was on the rise.

In the beginning, Mars Hill thrived within a "neighborhood context, operating with a strong theology of time and place,"[40] but over the years, their vision changed. With increasing notoriety, the church went multi-site, broadcasting Driscoll's messages to branches across four states.

Driscoll and his leadership team concentrated on expanding

publicity and impact. Their aggressiveness and drive enabled unprecedented influence. Driscoll published books, became a popular conference speaker, and launched Acts 29, a church-planting network.

Driscoll's fame around Seattle grew as well. The Mariners invited him to throw out the first pitch at a home baseball game. Driscoll also preached a gospel message at the Seahawks' massive coliseum.[41] The whole city knew who he was.

What was originally positive slowly moved in the wrong direction. One Mars Hill member said, "This all began as a work of the Spirit, but we quickly started to push harder and harder, trying to accomplish it with human efforts—bigger, better, faster, stronger."[42]

The qualities that took Mark Driscoll to the highest heights of modern evangelicalism were also what took him down. After years of spectacular growth, missteps undermined the enterprise. There were "charges of bullying" and "abusive behavior."[43] Offerings plummeted, and the church had to close branches and cut staff. Driscoll ultimately quit, writing the following in his resignation letter:

> I readily acknowledge I am an imperfect messenger of the gospel of Jesus Christ. There are many things I have confessed and repented of, privately and publicly . . . Specifically, I have confessed to past pride, anger, and a domineering spirit.[44]

Two weeks later, Mars Hill announced that it would dissolve. One of the largest evangelical churches in the Pacific Northwest ceased to exist.

Weakness in the local church can be terrible, but so can hubris. Laxity is a problem. Yet on the other side, arrogance and coercion can destroy beautiful institutions too. Leaders need to draw upon God's favor, not their own drive for advancement.

Mars Hill collapsed under the weight of its own cockiness and pretension. Bigger and stronger will not necessarily accomplish the most desirable goals. With a relentless drive for achievement, people are easily blinded. Growth should come honorably or not at all.

SAN CLEMENTE PRESBYTERIAN CHURCH

Leadership challenges can emerge with generational shifts and changing cultures. Sometimes those at the top will have to radically adjust their approaches to advance to another level.

An example of this is found in the story of San Clemente Presbyterian Church (SCPC) in Orange County, California. In 2007, under the leading of Tod Bolsinger, the congregation celebrated ten years of growth and a surplus of $100,000 in the general fund. He writes,

> We unified around a shared vision, and we had rebuilt our entire campus. We were starting big initiatives to serve our community, including planting a church, starting a community resource center and starting an additional Spanish-language service.[45]

Despite the church growth, Bolsinger and his team sensed that the momentum was fading. They wanted continued success, but the congregation lacked enthusiasm. Stagnation, after a season of sustained growth, was puzzling.

A consulting team was brought in and took SCPC through a point-by-point evaluation. At its conclusion, they confirmed that this congregation was one of the healthiest they had ever worked with. But the advisors wanted to discuss the unintended consequences of SCPC's leadership matrix. Bolsinger writes,

> The success of a unified vision had given birth to an overly centralized institution. The very unity, discipline and alignment needed to bring the church together to rebuild the campus around our vision were now stifling creativity, passion and energy.[46]

Pastor Tod Bolsinger was a visionary with inexhaustible zeal. This served the congregation well in the early days of his administration. But that leadership approach brought diminishing returns over time.

Kevin Graham Ford, a representative with the visiting consulting team, confessed the following to Bolsinger:

> Nobody thinks that you are trying to build the church around you, but that is, in fact, what is happening. Unconsciously, the message going out is that everybody here thinks it is their job to support the ministry that you are having here. And that model of leadership is out of date. It's a model from the past that is unsustainable in a changing world and is slowly sapping the passion from the church.[47]

Though SCPC was successful, the congregation was showing signs of wear. The previous paradigms weren't as attractive to those they were trying to reach. The families that they were serving were interested in a different mode of engagement.

The consultants advised Bolsinger to change his leadership approach. What gets a leader to one level often will not take them to the next. An old pastor used to tell me, "What got you here probably won't take you there. What God moves *in* is not necessarily what he will move *through*." This is some of the best counsel I have ever received.

Every new stage of development requires new modes of engagement. Growth is less common in ministry and in other enterprises because so few are willing to adapt. The Bible reminds us that old wineskins can't hold new wine (Matthew 9:14–17).

This is difficult, but senior pastors shouldn't hold too tightly to personal preferences. Instead, they should find the best way to missionally align and empower the next tier of leaders. What's best for the church might not be the most satisfying for the leader, but the good of the enterprise has to be the highest concern.

Churches fail when leaders aren't willing to grow and adapt. God has more for a congregation when the leaders are willing to press in and reassess. Sometimes leadership is simply about pivoting to a new modality. Change your stance—we either adapt or die.

DECLINING ATTENDANCE

I'm a hopeful man, but I recognize that the American church is struggling. I'm thankful for the growth occurring in Asia, Africa, and Latin America, but I'm saddened by the stagnation in the West.[48]

This enveloping religious crisis is demonstrated, in part, by declining church attendance. Apparently, participation has declined in 75 percent of US counties.[49] A short while ago, less than 18 percent of the American population attended a worship service on any given weekend.[50] The Gallup organization acknowledged this fact as well, saying: "The past 20 years have seen an acceleration in the drop-off, with a 20-percentage-point decline since 1999."[51]

Blogger and church analyst Carey Nieuwhof acknowledges that people are attending less frequently. He believes that this trend has been building for years. Nieuwhof writes,

> The issue has reached a tipping point in the church over the last decade . . . People who used to attend every week are attending three times a month. People who were around twice a month often

> now show up once a month. And attenders who used to come once a month are showing up half a dozen times a year.[52]

Families are not only attending less; many local fellowships are also sputtering out. Thom Rainer, looking at US stats, claims that nearly twenty churches close their doors every day.[53] Andy McAdams suggests that more than ten thousand churches disappeared over the last twenty years.[54] Preexisting congregations are shut down at double the rate that new ones can be established.

I don't even want to imagine the ramifications of COVID-19 in 2020–2021. I've seen some of the numbers, and statistics are much worse.

In many ways, the coronavirus pandemic has acted "as a 'force accelerant,' turbo-charging existing trajectories by a decade or more."[55] These types of disruptions will expose pre-existing problems.

LEADERLESS CHURCHES HAVE EMPTY PEWS

In this painful season, congregations are dealing with internal problems, but they are also facing outward obstacles. I already mentioned hostile local governments exploiting zoning laws. But politicians have become openly dismissive of churches. With the supposed goal of safety, they instituted far-reaching lockdowns. Tens of thousands of congregations could not gather for several months.

At least a dozen churches that I know of had to permanently shut down because of income losses and member attrition.[56] I wouldn't be surprised if there were thousands more.

All of this is happening in a context of intense social duress. Violent activists torched churches and charitable outreaches in Portland,[57]and government officials did little to assist them. In many places, congregations are dissuaded from protecting their properties. Many politicians seem to believe that Christianity is nonessential.

Leading through pandemics, riots, and other large-scale disasters is laborious, and mistakes occur. No one can control all the terrible forces at work in the world. Nevertheless, leaders have a responsibility to rise and take the helm of the ship. They have to find a way to navigate through the rough waters.

Multiple factors, such as political, economic, and cultural adversity, affect religious organizations. Selfishness and sin are also a part of the equation. Nevertheless, a crucial reason for ministry setbacks is poor leadership.

Without strategic leaders, there is no vision, and the congregants are less prone to attend weekly services. Deficient oversight will result in the exodus of members. Without insightful, Spirit-led rule, ministries will struggle to reach anyone. Leaderless churches have vacant pews.

Twenty-first century congregations need vision, purpose, and a connection to the Spirit of God. If we want things to change in the Western church, we must have leaders who are willing to lead with a strong hand.

WEAKNESS TO STRENGTH

Misery is often amplified through the failure of leadership. Negligence has destroyed businesses, agencies, and churches. Rudderless boats, tossed back and forth, will invariably crash on the rocks. Institutions fail without competent men and women at the helm.

Outcomes are rarely the product of outside forces. But we can't continue blaming our contemporary problems on a pandemic. This excuse is wearing thin. More often than not, an enterprise's culture and practices mirror the value system of its leader.

We must cut the clutter and reinstitute what's vital.

Organizations will teeter as they move beyond the foundations. Every leader wants to feel good about their contributions, but no one benefits from self-deception.

In a frustrating season, stories have the power to recenter us. They confront us and steer us to places we're hesitant to go. That happened to me years ago as I listened to Jim. This businessman's biblically infused narratives exposed some of my shortcomings. I'm eternally grateful for his storytelling.

First, we engage the stories, and then the stories have a way of engaging us. Often, uncomfortable friction points come into focus. The unfolding narratives force us to see issues we'd prefer to overlook and disrupt our skewed trajectories. The narratives provide new vantage points and opportunities for readjustment. The old stories often provide the groundwork for brave, new exploits.

The golden age has not passed. Even in difficult days, beautiful sagas are still being written. Let those who've gone before remind us that each generation can reimagine the world. Twenty-first century leaders don't have to govern like the failed bureaucrats of yesteryear. Our hands can be strong.

In every sphere of influence, a new breed is rising. These men and women are on the cutting edge of an inexplicable shift.

2

THE TENSION OF BEING AND DOING

I once tuned in to a speaker discussing leadership strategies. He was a skillful, well-polished panelist at a workshop. With a glistening, white smile, he spelled out the secrets of social media and how to hobnob with the affluent. This conference speaker positioned himself as a social media influencer. But not much turned up when I investigated his accomplishments. I found his follower count, photos, blog posts, and a few e-books. But he hadn't worked with anyone notable. The only thing that he achieved was turning himself into a media personality. This speaker was famous for being famous. He was a charming talking head but wasn't an actual leader. So many confuse theatrics with legitimate authority.

The meaning and scope of leadership are important. Analysts and authors talk endlessly about it, but I'm not sure that they're getting below the surface. Trending society has confused authority with fame and peripheral matters.

When leadership debates arise, people highlight particular points. For example, some will talk about servanthood, collaborative strategies, or a transformational approach to management. Church strategists and those working in the marketplace offer contrasting views. Some, in the political realms, will bring up the controversial critical race theory. People perceive leadership in radically different ways.

If you scroll through the selections on Amazon, you would find thousands of publications defining leadership. There is no scarcity of opinions about what it means and how it should be handled. Many of the teachings are profitable. Leaders would do well to hear the insights of others. We can learn from individuals with diverse backgrounds and practices. After all, even a broken clock is right twice a day.

Despite decent ideas, most evaluations are short-sighted. Many so-called leaders have been blinded by self-justification, tokenism, and cultural relevance. Typically, they're building a brand, not empowering a boots-on-the-ground organization.

As I share some of my convictions, I claim no expertise. While I've led a ministry organization, owned a business, and served as an associate pastor, I'm still a work in progress. I'm learning about leadership every day, and as my Arkansas relatives say, "I still have a ways to go."

In the following pages, I will share some of what I have learned over three decades. Please think of this as a few notes from my journey.

A TALE OF TWO LEADERS

As I talk about the meaning of leadership, I want to reduce it to two overlapping components. Before I explain this binary tension, I'd like to recount a modern parable.

Please consider how two leaders functioned in their spheres of authority. First, we see a youthful leader filled with excitement and a desire to engage. Reggie wasn't afraid to get his hands dirty and do what needed to be done. People were drawn to his passion and sense of mission. Reggie soon gathered many supporters.

However, a few years later, trouble arose. His immaturity and lack of experience began to show, and the people lost confidence in him. Some who were once excited about the organization started to disengage. They didn't feel as if they could follow a man who lacked stability.

Reggie went from being a fast-rising influencer to a forgotten figure in just a few short years. This young leader was *doing* plenty, but he was not *becoming* what his staff and supporters needed. Reggie needed to work more on his identity.

Now, we focus on a loyal and dependable older leader. He spent years building relationships. Brian was reliable and authentic. Everybody was convinced that this knowledgeable leader would take them into a bright tomorrow.

The ministry started beautifully, but a decade into Brian's leadership, the money dried up, and key people left the organization. They whispered behind closed doors that they didn't want to stay with a stagnant and irrelevant organization.

While the people wanted solid morals, they also wanted to be a part of a mission. This leader had character but was not accomplishing much.

In these stories, we observe two different leadership approaches. In the first, a young leader is driven by achievements. In the second, a leader is concerned with integrity. Both were partly correct but lacking all the puzzle pieces.

In the end, both Reggie and Brian failed because they didn't understand leadership resides in the tension of being *and* doing. It is about who you are *and* what you're accomplishing. When we bring both parts together and let them work in tension, this creates a powerful symbiosis.

We could talk about several leadership metaphors, but this tension provides one of the best windows into the mechanics of governance.

TENSION, NOT BALANCE

Leadership is in the ongoing tension between *being* and *doing*. These fluctuating dynamics are at play in everyone who is trying to establish a work.

Individuals seem to understand *balance* better than *tension*. Let me remind you that balance is bringing differing weights into equilibrium and making opposing sides equal.

Decades ago, in Greenwood, Arkansas, a teacher brought a hanging balance scale to her classroom. It had two metal arms with bowls attached on each side. As we learned about weights and measures, my classmates put apples, oranges, and grapes on the scale in an attempt to even out the arms. When I hear the term "balance," this is what I think of. But I'm not talking about *balance*; I'm talking about *tension*.

Tension is when two seemingly opposite forces pull against each other in varying degrees in give and take. As one part rises, the other falls. There is continual, synchronized interworking between the two. In the end, one finds the differing measures are appropriate to the needs.

Leadership is built on a tension that never entirely lets up. Individuals carry some of this *push* and *pull* into a lifetime of service.

GIDEON'S STRUGGLE

Jim, my entrepreneur friend, liked to tell Bible stories. He influenced me to pick up the habit. I want to draw upon the life-changing lessons in those ancient narratives whenever possible.

The account of the judge named Gideon in the Old Testament is a superb example of the tension of *being* and *doing*. As he came into his leadership position, he found a way to bring each of these elements together.

When the angel of the Lord first appeared to Gideon, he was

hunkered down in a winepress, hiding from the oppressive Midianites. Turmoil plagued the land, and he was hoping to thresh a little wheat to feed his family. Little did he know that he was about to be given the opportunity of a lifetime. "The angel of the Lord came and sat beneath the great tree at Ophrah . . . Gideon son of Joash was threshing wheat at the bottom of a winepress to hide the grain from the Midianites" (Judges 6:11 NLT).

As the angel conversed with Gideon, this complex leadership tension emerged. To move forward, he would have to grapple with both his identity and mission—*essence* and *effect*. Let's consider how this plays out.

GIDEON WRESTLED WITH HIS IDENTITY

As we begin our leadership journey, we have to figure out what stories we believe about ourselves. Over a lifetime, hundreds—family, friends, teachers, and politicians—are telling you who you are. Well-meaning people want to label you. That may all be well and good, but what is God saying?

Gideon is an example of the struggle for identity that resides in the heart of everyone. "When the angel of the Lord appeared to Gideon, he said, 'The Lord is with you, mighty warrior'" (Judges 6:12 NIV).

In this encounter, Gideon not only heard that God was "with him," but he also learned that he was a "mighty warrior." This claim probably seemed ridiculous. Gideon likely thought, *Where's God, and where is this so-called warring spirit?* Gideon had never fought anyone and was hiding in a winepress.

Despite these powerful declarations about his identity, the message didn't yet line up with reality. God often likes to speak the future ahead of time.

> The Lord turned to him and said, "Go with the strength you have, and rescue Israel from the Midianites. I am sending you!" "But Lord," Gideon replied, "how can I rescue Israel? My clan is the weakest in the whole tribe of Manasseh, and I am the least in my entire family!" The Lord said to him, "I will be with you. And you will destroy the Midianites as if you were fighting against one man." Gideon replied, "If you are truly going to help me, show me a sign to prove that it is really the Lord speaking to me." (Judges 6:14-17 NLT)

Although called to greatness, Gideon needed to overcome the issues squelching his destiny. Gideon rightly acknowledged that he was the weakest man from the weakest tribe in Israel. Many issues were standing in the way of his calling, but God positioned him to overcome every obstacle.

In this passage, we see a continual back and forth between *action* and *character development*. One kept feeding the other. As Gideon discovered who he was, he was positioned to act as a decisive leader.

GIDEON HAD TO LEARN TO ACT

As Gideon gained a stronger sense of who he was, he also had to learn how to execute the objectives assigned by the Lord. This was not just about his *essence* but also required *action*.

Gideon's response would ultimately come through tearing down the pagan altar of his father and driving out Israel's enemy, the Midianites.

- Tearing down the pagan altar of his father.
- Driving out Israel's enemy, the Midianites.

We have a lot to unpack in these two action points. Gideon felt a little anxious about these responsibilities. His internal struggles are similar to the conflicts that leaders go through today. What he learned is important for all of us to discover.

GIDEON TORE DOWN HIS FATHER'S ALTAR

Gideon was starting to grasp his identity when the Lord instructed him to tear down his father's altar. He would have struggled to act against a household shrine. Scattering the stones would have infuriated his family. He was undoubtedly uneasy by this.

Deep-rooted family issues often trap individuals. The anxiety and fears of parents are passed down to the rest of the family. Fathers should never be dishonored, but innocent sons are sometimes held back by generational constraints. This should never occur. The parent's ceiling should become the children's floor.

> That night the Lord said to Gideon, . . . "Pull down your father's altar to Baal, and cut down the Asherah pole standing beside it. Then build an altar to the Lord your God here on this hilltop sanctuary, laying the stones carefully" . . . So Gideon took ten of his servants and did as the Lord had commanded. But he did it at night because he was afraid of the other members of his father's household and the people of the town. (Judges 6:25-27 NLT)

The altars were leveled at night, with much trembling. Gideon was unsure of himself but acted anyway. He put these requirements above his own comforts. Overcoming inhibitions, Gideon placed his confidence in the all-consuming mission of God.

This decision moved Gideon into a whole new realm of engagement. The act of tearing down wicked family relics and breaking generational curses solidified his nobility and positioned him to accomplish a greater work in the days ahead.

GIDEON ATTACKED THE MIDIANITES

Gideon ultimately had to face a problem even more difficult than family disapproval. His character and emerging gifts would mean little if he couldn't deliver on the direst need.

"That night the Lord said, 'Get up! Go down into the Midianite camp, for I have given you victory over them!'" (Judges 7:9 NLT). Gideon, still working through the thorny issues of identity, was nervous about this weighty responsibility. How would he ever accomplish this feat?

This emerging warrior struggled, but through the Lord's leading, he was ready to execute an attack against the Midianites. The tension between *being* and *doing* was underway, and Gideon figured out how to make it work.

> When Gideon heard the dream and its interpretation, he bowed in worship before the Lord. Then he returned to the Israelite camp and shouted, "Get up! For the Lord has given you victory over the Midianite hordes!" [1]He divided the 300 men into three groups and gave each man a ram's horn and a clay jar with a torch in it. Then he said to them, "Keep your eyes on me. When I come to the edge of the camp, do just as I do. As soon as I and those with me blow the rams' horns, blow your horns, too, all around the entire camp, and shout, 'For the Lord and for Gideon!'" It was just after midnight, after the changing of the guard, when Gideon and the 100 men with him reached the edge of the Midianite camp. Suddenly, they blew the rams' horns and broke their clay jars. Then all three groups blew their horns and broke their jars. They held the blazing torches in their left hands and the horns in their right hands, and they all shouted, "A sword for the Lord and for Gideon!" Each man stood at his position around the camp and watched as all the Midianites rushed around in a panic, shouting as they ran to escape. (Judges 7:15-21 NLT)

In this dramatic story, an ordinary man had to grapple with the tensions of leadership. As he walked through this challenging ordeal, he not only clarified his calling but also executed more noble purposes.

Modern leaders need to follow his example. They must also work through the dynamics of *being* and *doing*. As you grapple with this tension, you are positioned to move up and out.

BEING

Leadership is inexplicably rooted in one's *being*. Like Reggie, the younger figure in the opening story, many talk about authority exclusively in *action terms*. Doing great things is undoubtedly part of the leadership quotient, but we also need to understand the importance of *identity*.

Leadership actually begins with who you are and what God is doing in you.

Leaders are unquestionably called to speak and act, but words and actions are clearly rooted in identity. Behavior exposes deeply entrenched *attitudes, experiences*, and *expectations*. A leader cannot escape the imprint of their essence.

Jesus reminded his early followers of this inexplicable truth. Drawing on poetic imagery, he shared the following:

> A good man, out of the good treasure of his heart, brings forth good. An evil man, out of the evil treasure of his heart, brings forth evil. For out of the abundance of the heart, his mouth speaks. (Luke 6:45 NIV)

Effective leaders find ways to press in, establishing *identity* and *purpose*. They advance in divine grace, understanding that leadership potential is determined by who they are *inside*.

Leaders should aspire to accomplish incredible feats, but the other side of this tension cannot be overlooked. Your influence is directly proportional to the quality of your character. *Essence* always precedes *effect*.

It takes a lifelong journey of personal development to become a transformative leader. This expanding drama involves an interchange between God and you. He brings his *favor*, and you respond with your *strength*. God empowers his leaders, and they learn to *embody* what he *empowers*.

IDENTITY

This process of development is difficult to navigate because most don't understand who they are or what constitutes their life. People tend to ignore what they find uncomfortable.

Many leaders don't seem to resolve the troubling emotional issues of their childhood. They don't realize that the past is still coloring their future. Some of what's been spoken over them has established impenetrable walls. So many on the front lines don't realize that their interior world inhibits their exterior world.

As long as a leader struggles with identity, he or she will have a hard time with healthy relationships and fruitfulness. Organizations will never reach their full potential as long as unresolved issues grip their teams.

I have observed first-hand how troubling personal issues hinder many in positions of authority. Some who are strong in public are a blubbering mess in private. They hide behind a façade.

Every leader, whether they acknowledge it or not, has weaknesses. But the inhibitors don't have to be an ongoing restriction. The story of Gideon teaches us that God has a way of enabling his children to rise from the shadows. God gives strength to the weak.

SONSHIP

God takes individuals who are alienated and alone and provides them with a place to belong. For the first time, they find a sense of identity and relational connection. God covers and embraces orphans with *unconditional love*.

The Lord transforms broken people into leaders by deeming them sons. Adopting hapless castaways, the Lord treats the outsider as his very own.

> Because you are his sons, God sent the Spirit of his Son into our hearts, the Spirit who calls out, "Abba, Father." So, you are no longer a slave, but God's child; and since you are his child, God has made you also an heir. (Galatians 4:6-7 NIV)

Much of this is rooted in the fact that humanity was called to be *image-bearers*. (See Genesis 1:26–28.) Men and women were made to demonstrate the heart and mind of the heavenly Father. Sin undermined this purpose, but Jesus's blood transforms everything. Because we're redeemed, we're now commissioned for mission.

One will never be an effective leader without learning to draw upon the joy of adoption. To go far, learn to walk in the spirit of sonship. Without this sense of identity, you will not be positioned to transform cultures.

A gifted leader took me aside once and said, "An essential part of establishing who you are is through understanding your place in the family of God. Jesus gives you confidence and stability through an emerging sense of identity. From this unshakable position, you can lead."

I will never forget his tone as he shared these words. I knew this was wisdom from someone who had traveled some challenging roads. I have tried to take that advice to heart.

I repeatedly see that a faithful son or daughter knows the way that the Father would go and is happy to take others in the same way. A deeply rooted identity is essential for effective leadership.

BITTER NO MORE

I'm dumbfounded at how a sense of *sonship* changes perception. A colleague of mine was constantly bitter. Scott grew up in a broken family and was alienated from his father at a young age. He had a tough time holding on to relationships and seemed to wear a perpetual scowl.

Somewhere along the way, Scott had an encounter with Jesus that altered his life. This formerly agitated man was revolutionized. A contentious kill-joy was suddenly a delight to have around.

I wasn't shocked when Scott later became a pastor. With this profound life-change, he reached out to hundreds, providing comfort and support. Scott brought individuals together in worship environments that I would have never anticipated. With his inexplicable joy, he probably could have planted a church in the darkest places in the world.

Scott recognized that he was a son in the kingdom of God, and this irrefutable truth brought him peace. The rejection he experienced from his biological father hurt less because he had now experienced the love of the heavenly Father. When Scott discovered who he was, he was positioned to help hundreds of others overcome their identity issues too.

When individuals embrace their position in the family of God, almost all issues are resolved. Meaningful connections and an understanding of sonship is an important catalyst for leadership.

CALLING

In addition to *sonship*, leadership is rooted in *calling*. I talked about this with a group of young adults, and one said, "What is that?" I told him that calling is a particular sense of mission that comes from God.

The pages of Scripture are filled with stories of individuals with extraordinary callings. God invited these men and women to partner with him in his purposes. Some of the leaders experiencing a dynamic calling includes the following:

- Abraham (Genesis 12:1-5)
- Moses (Exodus 3:1-12)
- Ruth (Ruth 1:15-18)
- Samuel (I Samuel 3:1-10)
- David (I Samuel 16:6-13)
- Esther (Esther 4:9-17)
- Jeremiah (Jeremiah 1:4-19)
- Mary (Luke 1:26-38)
- Lydia (Acts 16:11-15)
- Timothy (I Timothy 4:6-16)

Each accomplished remarkable feats, and their stories are intertwined in the larger narratives of the Bible. God also wants our stories to intersect with the enveloping story of redemption. Calling can be a powerful catalyst for mission.

Some think this part of the book won't apply to them because they feel no burden for ministry. But when I talk about calling, I'm referring to *vocation*. This is a sense of mission and purpose that undergirds everyone.

Only a few are called to full-time ministry. Most are empowered to function in business, government, education, or entertainment.

Individuals should pursue whatever God has called them to accomplish. We commend those who serve society and advance God's kingdom through business and other enterprises. Everyone needs to grasp what God has called them to do.

ERIC LIDDELL

In the Oscar-winning film, *Chariots of Fire*, we see an inspiring example of calling. I watched this movie as a boy, but I am still impacted by what it portrayed.

The motion picture tells the fascinating story of Eric Liddell, the "Flying Scot." While attending the University of Edinburgh, officials invited him to compete in the 1924 Olympics in Paris, France. In one of the crucial moments in the film, Liddell boldly declared, "God made me fast. And when I run, I feel his pleasure."[1] More driven than other students, he recognized the reason he was born.

Liddell competed in the four-hundred-meter dash in the Olympic Games, a race he was not favored to win. But he pushed beyond his shortcomings and won the gold medal. Liddell said, "The secret of my success over the 400 meters is that I run the first 200 as fast as I can. Then, for the second 200 meters, with God's help, I run faster."[2]

Liddell was stirred by what God planted inside him. As he ran, his soul surged with life. A sense of calling and purpose should also arouse our hearts. What do you do that causes you to feel God's pleasure?

BEYOND THE EXTERNALS

Callings don't necessarily operate the way people imagine. In fact, God is prone to work outside the box. Unlike humans, he's limitless and unencumbered. Society places too much weight on training or on the reasonable order of things. That may have some bearing, but it is only part of the equation.

God often operates outside the norm. Look at what he told the prophet Samuel as he was about to encounter a shepherd named David: "Do not consider his appearance or his height . . . The Lord does not look at the things man looks at. Man looks at the outward appearance, but the Lord looks at the heart" (1 Samuel 16:7 NIV).

David, who was small in build and the youngest of his family, went on to become the mightiest king in Israel. His destiny looked nothing like where it began. God often disrupts expectations as he establishes new patterns.

Divine calling is not about external markers but is rooted in the purposes God has established, which may be unknown or unseen. The Apostle Paul also declared this truth in the pages of the New Testament. He writes

> Remember, dear brothers and sisters, that few of you were wise in the world's eyes or powerful or wealthy when God called you. Instead, God chose things the world considers foolish in order to shame those who think they are wise. And he chose things that are powerless to shame those who are powerful. (1 Corinthians 1:26-27 NIV NLT)

Calling is not about acquired wisdom. Nor does it find itself rooted in nobility, strength, knowledge, or natural influence. Instead, calling is the flowering of the unique purposes God places inside an individual. This happens when one finally discovers what they were made to do.

MOTHER TERESA

When Anjezë Gonxhe Bojaxhiu, the youngest child of a poor Albanian immigrant family, was born, no one expected her to be a Nobel Lauriat or one of the iconic figures of the twentieth century.

From outward appearances, this fatherless, Catholic immigrant had little to offer the world, but within her was a vision for a great future. Stories of ancient missionaries and their sacrificial service inspired her. She wanted to do something substantial to help the poor.

After turning eighteen, she left her family and joined the Sisters of Loreto Convent. She took on the name Teresa, after Thérèse de Lisieux, the patron saint of missionaries. The world would later come to know her as Mother Teresa.

This frail woman traveled to India and began instructing the destitute. As Teresa witnessed the bitter scarcity in Calcutta, she realized that God was calling her to begin a work in that city. With meager resources, she established the Missionaries of Charity in 1950.

Teresa scribbled in her journal that her beginnings were fraught with misery. With no income, she scrounged for sustenance and resources. Uncertainty, loneliness, and a desire to return to the comforts of the convent nearly derailed her. She wrote

> Today, I learned a good lesson. The poverty of the poor must be so hard for them. While looking for a home I walked and walked till my arms and legs ached. I thought how much they must ache in body and soul, looking for a home, food and health. Then, the comfort of Loreto [her former convent] came to tempt me. "You have only to say the word and all that will be yours again," the Tempter kept on saying . . . Of free choice, my God, and out of love for you, I desire to remain and do whatever be your Holy will in my regard. I did not let a single tear come.[3]

Teresa's compassion and eagerness to display the sacrificial nature of Christ touched multitudes. She became recognized around the world for her work among the poor. Millions celebrated what a small Albanian nun accomplished in the slums of India. In 1979, Teresa received the Nobel Peace Prize for "work undertaken in the struggle to overcome poverty and distress."[4]

Teresa had started the Missionaries of Charity in Calcutta with only thirteen individuals, but by the time of her death in 1997, she had over four thousand people serving alongside her. The gifts within her compelled others to act.

Looks can be deceiving. Sometimes the powerless become the most powerful. Individuals that others are prone to write off may hold the key to transforming society. If God is no respecter of persons, then we shouldn't be either.

GIFTING

People talk about leadership in several different ways. Many tend to see it through an educational lens. The idea is, with superior curriculum or classes, better leaders will emerge. I've met hundreds who attended leadership training events with this goal. Obviously, aspects of this can be nurtured and developed. But leaders are rarely mass-produced.

Among the greats, an *x-factor*—a *je ne sais quoi*—an element hard to quantify determines outcome. The term "charisma" is often used to describe the impact of leaders. Those on the front lines often have inexplicable favor.

Over the years, historians have spoken of the charisma of Winston Churchill, Elvis Presley, and Ronald Reagan. Part of their influence can be attributed to their demeanor, speaking ability, or raw passion. They have an intangible something more, which explains this.

Authority is actually rooted in a giftedness that comes from God. This capacity aligns with higher purposes. Even unbelievers unknowingly possess gifts from the throne room of heaven.

For many, the term "charisma" connotes a compelling personality, which is the common English usage. But in the Bible, the term means an "infusion of grace." The word is sometimes connected to "spiritual gifts."

When discussing the *charismata,* or gifts of divine favor, people highlight: "wisdom, knowledge, discernment, faith, healing, miracles, prophecy, tongues and interpretation" (1 Corinthians 12:4–11). Many overlook the other gifts.

In another crucial passage, the apostle Paul documents other capacities. He writes, "We have different gifts, according to the grace given us. If a man's gift is . . . leadership, let him govern diligently" (Romans 12:6, 8 NIV).

This verse asserts that leadership is a gift from God. The ability to govern is just as much of a spiritual enabling as any modality. Authority cannot be reduced to a trained response.

In this discussion, another passage is important to consider. It refers to leadership as a *spiritual impartation*: "In the church, God has appointed . . . leadership skills (1 Corinthians 12:27–28 CEB). This phrase is sometimes translated as "gifts of administration." The original phrasing suggests "governance" or "decision-making," which are clearly abilities God appoints.

Based on these passages, I would say that *leadership is a supernatural grace that comes at the discretion of God. It is a divine enablement that fundamentally changes the essence of a person.*

As God *gifts* an individual, they have the potential to embody his purposes. This grace affects the recipient at the core of who they are.

I want to acknowledge one other point. If leadership is a spiritual gift, not everyone possesses it. Some become irritated when I say this, but not all are equally capable of leading.

While all have been gifted in some way, not all have been graced with the ability to govern. Individuals need to celebrate what God gives and not quibble over what is supposedly missing. In order to serve best, stay in your lane. Embody what you are entrusted with.

Leadership is an outworking of grace and favor, not a product of education, manipulation, or self-promotion. One cannot operate in a gift that they don't actually possess. Society needs to re-embrace the value of giftings. Leaders are more than an organizational or cultural construct. They are endued with grace.

DEVELOPMENT

As we discuss the notion of *becoming* a leader, here is another important aspect. Many mistakenly believe leadership is activated as soon as one is *called*. They think that one can start governing immediately. This is rarely true.

Effective leaders usually emerge after an extended period of development. The grace usually comes to fruition over time.

- Joseph had to go through an extended season of slavery and imprisonment before he rose to a position of prominence (Genesis 37-48).
- Moses spent forty years as a fugitive before he was ready to lead the people out of Egypt (Exodus 2:11-4:17).
- Joshua served for more than forty years before he became Moses's successor (Exodus 17:8-16; Numbers 13:16-17; 14:22-24; Joshua 1:1-9).
- Elisha served Elijah for many years before he took on his master's mantle and became a great prophet (1 Kings 19:19-21; 2 Kings 2:1-14).
- The disciples spent more than three consecutive years training with Jesus before they emerged as leaders of the early church (Gospels and Acts).
- Paul became the apostle to the Gentiles seventeen years after His initial experience on the road to Damascus (Acts 9:1-31; Acts 13:1-14:28; Acts 16:1-28:31; Romans 1:5).

Many called to lead don't understand that developing as a leader is a process. In leadership spheres, there are no overnight successes. Identity and character have to be developed. Strength typically comes with time. No one can rush it.

MICHAEL JORDAN

Like many men my age, I was enthralled with Michael Jordan—basketball star and late twentieth-century cultural icon. While playing for the Chicago Bulls, his soaring leaps and graceful athleticism captivated the nation.

My buddies had posters depicting Jordan dunking the ball from across the court—tongue hanging out. He was universally acclaimed as "the greatest basketball player of all time."[5]

It's tough to imagine that such a pacesetter had to undergo a period of personal development. But even the exceptional Michael Jordan went through this.

When Jordan attended Emsley A. Laney High School in Wilmington, North Carolina, he didn't make the varsity basketball squad. One of the world's greatest athletes was thought to be too short and unskilled to play.

Michael Jordan cut? That's the kind of claim that my high school buddies and I would have found implausible. But it actually happened. At that stage in his life, he wasn't quite ready to play.

Excluded from the team, Jordan rigorously trained, engaging in the fundamentals. He shot a hundred free throws every day. He took a basketball to bed with him each night. He'd practice getting a perfect backspin before shutting his eyes. Over the months, Jordan improved substantially.

Naturally, everything was different at the start of the next basketball season. Jordan was much wiser and faster. He discovered new channels to unlock his innate talent within. Needless to say, Jordan made the team and began to dominate his opponents.

Jordan received a scholarship for the University of North Carolina and later became a breakout star for the Chicago Bulls, winning six championships. I told a younger colleague, "LeBron James and every other player in the NBA are still trying to play catch-up with Michael Jordan." He rolled his eyes at me, and we both laughed.

Most people are drawn to excellence. It's easy to forget that even the greatest talents don't initially shine out of the starting gate. It takes time to develop into an extraordinary person. Leadership, on the courts and in other avenues, rarely shows up overnight.

Delays are not necessarily negative. They can deepen one's determination and position them to face other obstacles. Leaders often emerge in strength after a challenging wilderness experience.

KING DAVID

We struggle when we walk through gut-wrenching character development. Most don't want to go through it. They don't understand what's actually occurring in the *stretch*. Emerging leaders have rarely examined what it means to wrestle with the process of preparation.

In many ways, King David in the Old Testament provides excellent insight into this challenging process. While David was anointed as king as a young man, he had to wait twenty years before ruling over the tribes. Most don't have that kind of patience. They feel a compulsion to seize power as soon as possible. David refused to give in to that kind of temptation.

At one point, Saul, the monarch terrorizing David, was crouching in a cave. David had an ideal opportunity to enact a blow and take the crown. He could have ended it all, but he decided he wouldn't seize power dishonorably. Instead, he was willing to patiently wait on God for his promotion. (See 1 Samuel 24.)

David's willingly allowed the Lord to form him, which enabled him to become a transformative leader in the ancient world. He gave the Lord room to work as he saw fit. Centuries later, we still describe David as "a man after God's own heart."

CHARACTER DETERMINES REACH

A lot of situations are framed incorrectly. Individuals on the front lines must understand that their authority flows from their identity. Who one is expands or restrains their influence. Character often defines reach.

While God gives you a sense of calling and purpose, he invites you to be involved in the process of maturation. Identity is often solidified through interchanges between heaven and Earth.

God is implementing his purposes, but you're willingly participating in this adventure. The Spirit is initiating, and you're learning how to respond. Who you are rises from these interactions. All that you do will intersect with who you are.

REHOBOAM

While evaluating what it means to become a leader, we can consider biblical stories where individuals wrestled with difficulties. As I said, my business-minded friend inspired me to do this.

We already discussed a few examples from the life of David, but we can also reflect on the experiences of his grandson, Rehoboam.

Just before Rehoboam's reign, his father, Solomon, had made it hard on Israel. He wanted his nation to be the greatest on Earth. But Solomon was fulfilling this dream on the backs of the citizens.

Taxes were high, and the citizens spent a vast amount of time working in construction. Though loyal subjects, they had been reduced to slaves.

As the youthful Rehoboam took the throne, the people made a simple request. "'Your father was a hard master,' they said. 'Lighten the harsh labor demands and heavy taxes that your father imposed on us'" (1 Kings 12:4 NLT).

Rehoboam contemplated their concerns and sought guidance from his father's counselors. These men had been in leadership positions for years and had wisdom. "If you are willing to be a servant to these people today and give them a favorable answer, they will always be your loyal subjects" (1 Kings 12:7 NLT).

Unlike Rehoboam, the older counselors understood what was taking place in the kingdom. Because of their knowledge of the people, they knew what was advantageous. Despite Rehoboam's position and power, he did not yet have wisdom. Rather than listening to the advice of the elders, he entertained the counsel of his friends. His peers said,

> This is what you should tell those complainers who want a lighter burden: "My little finger is thicker than my father's waist! Yes, my father laid heavy burdens on you, but I'm going to make them even heavier! My father beat you with whips, but I will beat you with scorpions!" (1 Kings 12:10–11 NLT)

Unfortunately, Rehoboam didn't see his own youth and inexperience. He didn't understand that his leadership was inhibited by immaturity. He embraced the foolish counsel of friends and followed in the footsteps of his father.

When the people of Israel recognized Rehoboam's unreasonable choice, they grew enraged. "When all Israel realized that the king had refused to listen to them, they responded, 'Down with the dynasty of David!'" (1 Kings 12:16 NLT).

Understanding Rehoboam's leadership stance, ten of the Israeli tribes refused to continue the alliance. They walked away. The king's deficiency of character helped stir the fires of rebellion.

What should have been his moment of triumph instead became a moment of shame. Rehoboam, not knowing who he was, overextended his reach and lost the kingdom. History definitely provides poignant lessons.

INTERNAL CONSTITUTION

Leadership is rooted in an individual's underlying sense of being. Sadly, multitudes derail their own advancement because of an unwillingness to work on their lives. Oblivious to their own deficiencies, they make moves that alienate followers and undermine their organizations. Influence is shipwrecked through cantankerous impulses and immaturity.

One's sphere of authority is determined, in part, by their inner constitution. What's *within* invariably comes *out*—shaping environments and culture. Character sets the tone and colors conversations. Over the years, I've repeatedly heard an old Latin proverb: "It is absurd that a man should rule others, who cannot rule himself." Self-regulation and internal growth position an individual to reach the next level.

DOING

Identity sets the bar for leadership. What's beneath the surface manifests in inexplicable ways. Yet the underpinnings aren't the only determining factor. Let's consider another aspect and explore the other side of this leadership tension.

Governance isn't just positional; it's also functional. It's more than what one *represents*; it's also what is *done*. People can become so caught up in the *who* that they forget the *what*. We need both parts of this fully activated.

Some are like Brian, the older leader mentioned in the early part of this chapter. They've laid all the foundations and formed the right relationships. Yet when it's time to act, they hesitate.

An individual who is reluctant to act isn't a leader. Speaking to this concern, the apostle Peter urged his followers to "prepare your minds for action" (1 Peter 1:13). This spiritual father knew that it is vital to imagine and fully enact the purposes of God.

RESPONSIBLE

Leaders achieve outcomes, and pivotal to this is their sense of responsibility. Because of continued demands, innovators are ready to graciously respond. Genuine authority is rooted in the willingness to maintain cohesiveness and lighten the burdens of others.

Anytime tension builds and circumstances begin to unravel, the responsible ones feel a duty to bring restoration. They instinctively work to right wrongs and ensure that situations flow efficiently.

Leadership isn't about seizing power or establishing the rules; it's about serving others. Those genuinely *called* grasp this. They know people aren't placed into positions of authority to throw their weight around or boss underlings. They have arisen because of a willingness to carry the load. They are obligated to preserve and protect the community.

It comes down to this: If you aren't willing to pay the price and take responsibility for others, you're in no position to lead. A title or position mean very little if you aren't ready to manage difficulties. Leadership could be described as a *sense of responsibility* in the *hands of capable individuals*.

DEACONS

One of the clearest depictions of *leadership as responsibility* comes from the pages of the Bible. In the first century, problems increased as the church grew. Social and cultural fissures naturally come to the surface with rapid growth.

To ensure that the church ran smoothly, some gifted men were appointed by the apostles to step in and take care of the deficiencies. They were called deacons. "Choose seven men from among you who are known to be full of the Spirit and wisdom. We will turn this responsibility over to them" (Acts 6:2–3 NIV).

The deacons weren't only laborers and support team members. They took on the burden of managing community affairs.

In this passage, their leadership role was understood as embracing responsibility. This is about more than having a likable personality or utilizing effective oratory; authority is based on duty.

PRESIDENT HARRY S. TRUMAN

Harry S. Truman, the improbable thirty-third President of the United States, maintained that leadership was a resolute trust. He once famously stated that whoever was in charge "has to decide. He can't pass the buck to anybody."[6]

"Passing the buck" was an old gambler's term, used to describe the dealer's responsibility to distribute the cards and setup the game. After that hand was completed, the dealer would "pass the buck" to the next player, who would lead the next round.

When Truman used this term, he was saying that he wouldn't dodge his responsibilities. He was prepared to be accountable for everything within his leadership sphere. The president was declaring, "I will take the blame for everything."

To drive this sentiment home, Truman had a wooden sign created for his desk that read, "The buck stops here."[7] This cantankerous Missouri politician was willing to be on the hook for everything. In fact, he made it his motto.

Like Truman, legitimate leaders are willing to take responsibility —even for messes they didn't make. They refuse to grumble or blame anybody for the mishaps. They roll up their sleeves and try to work out problems.

Leaders are responsible. They're prepared to stay up late and persist to the end when called for. Like compassionate mothers and fathers, they voluntarily embrace the obligations, no matter how tedious. It's how they hold the family together and keep the ball rolling.

WINSTON CHURCHILL

As the ravages of World War II intensified in the late 1930s, the armies of the United Kingdom were facing what appeared to be a hopeless fight against Germany.

Winston Churchill, the impassioned prime minister, took to the Parliament floor and the radio airwaves to rouse the people. He once told the *House of Commons*, "Let us, therefore, brace ourselves to our duties, and so bear ourselves that if the British Empire and its Commonwealth last for a thousand years, men will still say, 'This was their finest hour.'"[8]

Churchill took responsibility for England's destiny. He inspired and mobilized his countrymen in the face of uncertainty. In many ways, Churchill provided the decisive leadership that kept England from falling into the clutches of the German war machine.

Churchill is an example of what it means to take responsibility as a leader. When others began to talk about peripheral matters, Churchill reminded them, "The price of greatness is responsibility."[9]

True leaders are willing to bear the terrible burden of the mission. They know that someone has to be responsible for the lives of the people. They aren't willing to stand back while everything falls apart. A sense of responsibility compels them to act.

JOHNSON & JOHNSON

In the fall of 1982, a batch of Tylenol capsules poisoned seven individuals in the Chicago-metro area. Apparently, someone tampered with the bottles at the factory, lacing the pills with potassium cyanide.

Although not at fault, the Johnson & Johnson company assumed responsibility for what transpired. The CEO set up a toll-free hotline and recalled thirty million bottles of Tylenol capsules—valued at more than one-hundred million dollars.

In addition to removing products from the market, the company issued detailed warnings to hospitals and health-care providers. The board of directors collaborated with the Chicago Police Department, the FBI, and the Food and Drug Administration.

Johnson and Johnson took out full-page newspaper ads, asking families to not consume their products. They also offered to swap out Tylenol capsules already in homes with new tablets.

At the time of this crisis, Johnson & Johnson was reeling. The company's market share tumbled from 35 percent to 8 percent. Analysts didn't believe that this beloved brand could survive the crisis.

But Johnson & Johnson faced the biting criticisms head-on with press conferences and public engagement. They led the way by advocating for new safety measures and triple-sealed medicine packaging. They made appeals to Congress to pass anti-tampering laws. They refused to hide in their darker moments.

Johnson & Johnson responded to this crisis in an exemplary manner. Since the leaders took responsibility, the company rebounded in less than a year.[10] Sometimes crises arise due to no fault on the part of the organization. But leaders can't sit back when trouble comes. They have to be responsible for everything, including tragedies.

PRODUCTIVE

In addition to the magnitude of responsibility, we have other factors to consider. When people talk about God's commands, they usually discuss several things, for example, love and compassion. Others will point out prayer and reading the Bible. I understand why these would come to mind when describing God's commands. Each of these are vital.

However, one responsibility is rarely acknowledged—productivity. This neglect is a shame because it's rooted in the original mission God gave humankind.

The initial command of Scripture to the man and the woman was tied to the importance of fruitfulness. The Lord declared, "Be fruitful and increase in number. Fill the earth" (Genesis 1:28 NIV).

The heavenly Father made it clear that he expects his sons and daughters to be productive. This command involved more than birthing children. As his "image-bearers" (Genesis 1:26), we're called to demonstrate all of who God is within the natural order.

This overarching purpose hasn't changed over the centuries. God still expects his leaders to be fruitful on the earth. We have been called to become producers. Reflecting on this, Jesus declared,

> Those who remain in me, and I in them, will produce much fruit. For apart from me you can do nothing . . . When you produce much fruit, you are my true disciples. This brings great glory to my Father. (John 15:5, 8 NLT)

In this passage, Jesus says that the fruit they bear confirms the servants of God. A barren individual would not have been noteworthy in the first century. They would prefer to consider the claims of the fruitful.

SYMBOLISM OVER SUBSTANCE?

Many in contemporary America have a different outlook on productivity, which isn't a major concern. Culturally, an increasing number of people minimize the importance of fruitfulness.

Some of this may be a backlash against the Baby Boomers (1944-1964). To overgeneralize, the post–World War II generation was all about building institutions, and they expected their kids and grandkids to follow this same pattern. But Gen-X (1965–1980), Millennials (1981–1996), and Gen-Z (1997–2021) had other worries. They were busy wrestling with anxiety and a declining job market. For younger generations, resolving identity issues became a greater burden. Productivity is not high on their list of priorities.

When we track generational tensions, we can see other patterns unfolding. In this cultural climate, social media drives people to obsess over *form* and *technique*, not actual *outcomes*. How a matter is framed is a preeminent concern.

Some, for example, don't grade a film on pacing, cinematography, or script. The only concern for them is the diversity of the cast. Equity and fair-mindedness are relevant, but virtue signaling, pandering, or tokenism is not necessarily the same as creative output.

Politics, movies, fashion, and music—the zeitgeist of the age—grips the imagination of myriads. But we must entertain the voices of dissent. A more honest voice should say that posturing means surprisingly little. Looking beyond methods and style, someone has to actually deliver the goods. A leader needs to warn society about the pitfalls of valuing symbolism over substance.

If we want to see global changes, we must return to our foundational purposes. We were designed to be mighty in word and deed as we walk in the footsteps of Jesus. Humans were intended to be fruitful on the earth.

Productivity may not be fashionable, but creators will have more to say in the end. Substance always wins over style in the long game.

DILIGENT

It's hard work to hold an enterprise together. The leadership role requires that person to go the extra mile. Authority figures should be diligent in their efforts. World changers aren't afraid to take risks.

I know a young entrepreneur who considered investing in a fast-food franchise. Rather than believing the company's grandiose claims, Jeremy did his own research. He told me, "I had to do my due diligence."

After examining all the data, Jeremy backed out of the deal. His willingness to thoroughly research kept him from making a bad financial decision.

Leadership is exhibited in one's eagerness to run beyond the finish line. It's not just *who you are* and *what you do*, but also *how you do it*. World changers are willing to go as far and as fast as necessary.

The apostle Paul speaks of this, writing, "If a man's gift is . . . leadership, let him govern diligently" (Romans 12:6, 8 NIV). This passage makes a simple declaration: If you're a leader, lead forcefully and passionately. This responsibility calls for diligent execution. Mere acts are not adequate; they need to be performed with *exuberance*.

If an individual has received a leadership gift, they should discharge every duty they have been entrusted with. There are no excuses for laxity or inaction. Those in charge should be ready to brandish their strength.

Over the years, I've spoken with passive leaders. Even in the most basic decisions, they hesitated. They were so afraid of making a mistake that they didn't put much effort into shaping the community. They had no real drive.

Even if naysayers openly criticize leaders, they shouldn't be afraid to exert their callings. They are hardwired to overcome obstacles. Pacesetters determine direction and diligently advance into the great unknown.

ULYSSES S. GRANT

In the early stages of the Civil War, the northern armies possessed superior manpower and equipment. Nevertheless, they were soundly defeated in battle. As previously discussed, the Union soldiers were hampered by ineffective leadership. Something had to change if the Union would be preserved.

Ulysses S. Grant was not the best-educated or talented of the Union officers. In fact, he brawled with fellow soldiers and struggled with drunkenness. Grant had his flaws. Yet the general had a quality that others did not possess—determination.

As soon as Lincoln made him commander, Grant was already positioned to act. In the fog of war, he valiantly advanced, unleashing the full might of the northern armies. Grant was willing to pay the unimaginable cost to be victorious.

It wasn't glamorous, but fortitude and grit enabled Grant to triumph on the battlefield. With his unwavering resolve, the tide turned. Within a relatively short period, the Civil War was finally brought to an end.

Ulysses S. Grant is an example of what might occur when a leader is willing to get his hands dirty. Thousands of critics might second-guess your moves. You might even suffer bloodshed and loss, but victory is only seized by those who are willing to swing the sword.

ACCESSIBLE

Along with other duties, a leader should also be accessible. This can be awkward and inconvenient, but authorities who make themselves available transform institutions.

Thought leaders, high-level politicians, or multi-national CEOs might be exceptions, but leadership is usually localized within a particular community. Authority becomes ingrained in real-world relationships and conversations. Remove these components, and you lack connection.

Many think of leadership as securing a respected title or mastering a competency. With this mindset, subordinates defer to a position or to expertise. But this old-fashioned notion is detached from others and reliant on external indicators.

Oratory, *rituals*, and *traditions* truly shape institutions. *Speeches*, *writing*, or *symbolic acts* can influence individuals. However, rhetoric and gestures only take a leader so far.

Thumbing their noses at older models, twenty-first century teams want leaders to break away and come alongside them. Time constraints or other subtleties don't concern teams. They don't care about other dynamics; they seek accessibility from their up lines.

In earlier generations, leaders separated and segregated. They justified lofty positions by being above the fray. This understanding still carries some validity. Authorities shouldn't get caught up in social media arguments or behave like insolent children. They must assert a certain decorum, but in the long run, personal distance rarely creates meaningful connections.

Western culture is drifting away from hierarchal models. People no longer see the world through the lens of *who is over who*. For most, titles no longer have relevance. In fact, myriads are skeptical of so-called experts. In the post-pandemic era, many question official government reports. People are more comfortable relying on friends for opinions and answers.

In most circles, leadership capital is no longer derived from knowledge, competencies, or even conferred titles. Instead, it comes from engagement and meaningful connection. The equity a leader receives in this hour is from his or her associations.

Leaders mired in outdated mindsets are discovering that it's tough to bring about change through speeches, written policies, or emails. I've found several helmsmen shocked that a command-and-control approach wasn't fruitful.

Let me reiterate, detached leadership methods no longer work, and I'm not certain that they ever did. Individuals were previously prone to put up with more because they had fewer choices. If they wanted access to opportunities, they had to go along with established structures. But we live in a day where the paradigm is changing. Possibilities are expanding. Some lieutenants are jumping ship and identifying new generals to serve under.

Leaders are discovering that if they don't find ways to better engage subordinates, they will forfeit the right to speak into their lives. It comes down to this: One can't effectively lead if they never work side-by-side with their teams. World-changers have to come down from their ivory towers and get into the trenches.

So many factors affect this. When a leader doesn't stay in touch with what's happening, they lose the pulse of the organization. They make decisions that don't consider what's happening on the ground.

Accessible leaders make a real difference. They are close to the heartbeat of the enterprise.

SAM WALTON AND WALMART

In 1988, my dad took me to the grand opening of the Sam's Club in Fort Smith, Arkansas. While there, I interacted with Sam Walton, the CEO of Wal-Mart. Though small in build, he was larger than life. Walton wore a tailored gray business suit and a cheap trucker cap—a bizarre contrast. The hat and the suit mirrored his unique life. Although Walton was a wealthy businessman, he was also a man of the people.

When I went in, Walton shook my hand, looked me in the eye, and spoke directly to me. He seemed genuinely interested in my feedback. This CEO laughed with the cashiers and listened to his customers. In fact, Walton carried an audio recorder in his pocket, dictating observations. He knew that for his business to prosper, he had to stay rooted in the real world.

Later, I heard other Walmart employees reminisce about their boss. They felt that he cared about them and wanted to hear their concerns. Although he was the multimillionaire CEO of the largest retail chain in the United States, he remained approachable.

Walton saw the value of graciously engaging the common man. Apparently, some of the company's greatest innovations came from what Sam learned while visiting stores. Perhaps one of the reasons Walmart became so successful was because of the accessibility of Sam Walton.

MORE THAN AN OPEN DOOR POLICY

This goes without saying, but the more responsibility a leader takes on, the less available they are. Organizational planning, appointments, staff meetings, and crisis management tend to quickly fill the calendar slots.

I'm not suggesting that leaders abandon all tasks and responsibilities for relationship building. That kind of decision would be disastrous. But I'm suggesting that they make room for what matters.

Effective leaders communicate with their teams and ensure that processes work. They also help make the long-term patterns of engagement clear. More than making a vague open-door policy, efficient leaders make it known when and how they can be reached.

They recognize that they can't talk to everybody but make ample time for meaningful dialogue.

A leader should maintain healthy boundaries around their time, energy, and attention but should not overlook other important matters. Disruptive engagement can fuel innovation and growth. Leaders can then easily network, access information, elicit feedback, and advance the values of the enterprise.

ACCOUNTABLE

Leaders *do* and *go*. They're innately *productive, responsible, diligent,* and *accessible*. But there's another component—*accountability*. No matter how fast or far a pioneer runs, they remain answerable to the mission and the organizational stakeholders. Power divorced from partnership, covenant relationship, and accountability will often result in disaster.

A leader must have an internal compass—an unassailable integrity. But they're accountable for more than just their own sense of mission. The pacesetters must ensure they leave a better future for those behind them. They recognize that as they step into uncharted territories, they're clearing paths for sons and daughters.

Nathan, one of my Canadian friends, told me that when he takes his toddlers out in the snow, he makes his footprints as large as possible because his kids use them to walk through the slush. He knows the challenges and acts accordingly. He's accountable for the well-being of his children.

Leaders are also responsible to their peers and overseers, even if this is not formally established. No man is an island. His attitude and actions impact the whole community.

Those in charge understand that they have to answer for their tactics in good times and bad. They're held to a higher standard. Whether verbalized or not, others often ask these questions:

- Do the attitudes and actions align with organizational values?
- How are we accomplishing the vision?
- What results are we producing?

Team members scrutinize choices, behaviors, and actions, and leaders are responsible for outcomes. Leaders face internal and external pressure points. No matter how high one is in the chain of command, they answer to someone or something.

Sometimes no one has enough clout to hold a leader accountable. That is why self-governance is so vital. Those who hold themselves in check seldom have to deal with a mutiny.

THE LAX FOOTBALL COACH

My high school football coach from Greenwood, Arkansas, instituted some harebrained plays and refused to motivate the players. When conditions became difficult, he withdrew from everybody. He forgot that he was accountable to his players and to many others in the town.

With his lack of engagement, the players increasingly turned against each other, and the situation worsened. The most capable team my town ever had didn't even make it to the playoffs. The coach's failure to invest in the team undermined our potential.

There's no way around it; organizations rise or fall because of those at the helm. Leadership matters. People in authority will invariably determine the trajectory and impact of an enterprise.

Accountable leaders are prepared to say, "I'm sorry" when they make mistakes or when plans go awry. They provide viable solutions. These leaders are not afraid to repair broken systems or make corrections and willingly clean up their messes.

A strong sense of accountability builds trust and establishes a culture of honor in an organization. In this, fairness and reasonable standards are established. Shared values enable everyone to advance together.

WILLINGNESS TO EXECUTE

Leadership is not about being the most glamorous or popular. It is not about performing perfectly or avoiding every mistake. Rather, leaders willingly execute what's needed for as long as necessary.

Action is essential. Society isn't asking for any more theorists and talking heads. They're crying out for forerunners who accomplish what needs to be done. They want people who take action.

Even in the face of hardships and opposition, leaders find ways to faithfully execute. The passionate ones can't stand on the sidelines; they are ready to move ahead. They won't rest until they see everyone mobilized.

If you don't willingly act, you cannot truly be called a leader. Genuine authorities know they must sometimes run crosscurrent with the world. They desire to be on the forefront of a societal shift.

THE PUSH AND THE PULL

A young leader once asked me if the struggle ever ends. I told him that it doesn't as long as you're on the front lines. I explained that a leader continually toggles between *identity* and *activation*. Progress is rooted in the *who* and the *what*. This underlying *push* and the *pull* unfold in varying intervals. *Authority* is embedded in both the *essence* and the *effect*.

Rather than finding balance, a leader's goal is to manage the tension. Authentic authority emerges in the interplay between *being* and doing. Few maintain a symbiosis for very long. Changing circumstances demand readjustments. The pressure points never entirely leave. Leadership often happens in the stretch.

I've had to grapple with this over the last few decades. Insecurities and identity issues hindered my development—and sometimes still do. But as I processed through the pain and learned to engage, this revolutionized my leadership. As my *being* and *doing* came more in sync, I progressively gained more influence.

In the Old Testament, after succeeding Moses, Joshua was forced to come to grips with his God-given identity: "Be strong and courageous, for you are the one who will lead these people to possess all the land" (Joshua 1:6 NLT). Moses's second-in-command was becoming *something* so that he could accomplish *everything*.

Joshua had to draw on a new sense of strength so that the people would press through against insurmountable barriers. He, like many other pioneers, discovered that what's *inside* enables what's *outside* to arise.

Leadership begins *within*, but execution is also vital. Action can often open the door to personal growth. These two elements are interconnected.

Being and *doing* will always be in tension, but these points don't have to cause a breakdown. A developing leader learns to manage both realms simultaneously. Identity and action don't have to be mutually exclusive.

Jesus, in his messianic role on Earth, was "mighty in deed and word before God and all the people" (Luke 24:19 ESV). He said and did wonderful things because every sphere was in alignment. Jesus's right relations with his heavenly Father and his countrymen created a context for fruitfulness.

Jesus came to the earth to be an example for humanity. He said, "Everyone who is fully trained will be like his teacher" (Luke 6:40 ISV). We can and should imitate Jesus's unique blend of *being* and *doing*.

Who are you before God and others? In what way are you

processing the tension points that emerge? How you respond will dictate your future. Your life is often a product of your own choices.

For me, grappling with the *push* and the *pull* has been more complicated than I expected. I've gone through fruitful periods—feeling as if I were ready to change the world. I was expecting a new project or responsibility when I was unexpectedly forced into a *season of introspection*. Suddenly, I needed to focus on character development and the rebuilding of relationships. That wasn't the direction I expected to go. Circumstances can shift very quickly, and you will need to be ready to pivot. In the long run, these tensions will strengthen you in the same way that strong winds solidify the root system of a tree.

In order to align your interior and external world, you will need to intentionally focus on this fundamental aspect of personal development. Responsibilities and the circumstances of life will provide opportunities for fine tuning. A called one is *tempered* through this ongoing process.

Your *identity* prepares you for *activation*. But periodically, you will not walk into a position until after you inaugurate your plan. This might sound backward, but *in doing*, you *become*.

The numerous capacities that you're bringing into your life will often transform you on the inside. The *push* and *pull* never entirely ends. You will have to repeatedly *process* changes.

Leaders have to contend with who they are and what they're carrying out. As they wrestle out the complications of *identity* and *action*, they pay the price to create beauty in this world. (See Philippians 2:12.) A failure to process this tension will invariably slow momentum and stifle fruitfulness.

As God-ordained leaders embrace *sonship* and *calling*, they are enthusiastically laboring in revelation from the realms of heaven. With a healthy sense of identity and a readiness to act, they disrupt darkness and transform the world.

Leadership emerges when *essence* and *effect* find resonance. Tod

E. Bolsinger writes that leadership is "about transformation and mission, about growing and going, about personal development and corporate effectiveness—all simultaneously."[11] We must understand the reality of leadership. These fundamentals are constant in feast or famine—in crisis or in peace.

Yes, the world is in upheaval, but that shouldn't stop the momentum of the kingdom. It's time for twenty-first-century leaders to change the world. They can do this by learning to navigate the challenging tension of *being* and *doing*.

3

LEADERSHIP MECHANICS

Over the years, the leadership abilities of a high school English instructor inspired me. Amber's dedication to the transformational possibilities of the classroom filled me with hope. Although she never thought of herself in these terms, she is one of the brightest leaders that I know.

A big part of what impressed me are the multi-dimensional aspects of Amber's leadership. She could toggle between several responsibilities throughout the workday. This woman truly knew how to use multiple tools to impact the lives of kids.

This educator was empathic, charming, and communicative. She knew how to motivate distracted students and spur them into action. Her classroom was organized, and kids felt safe there.

Teachers try to reach awkward teenagers and help them get their lives together, a difficult task indeed. But she did it every day with grace. This teacher taught me that legitimate authority requires quick thinking, wisdom, and emotional intelligence.

In one of our conversations, I told her that she was exceptional, but she shrugged it off, saying:

> I'm nothing special. I'm just doing my job. Young people are our nation's future, and we must do all that we can to help them. What other purpose is there? Educators must guide the next generation forward.

Amber regularly identified students' giftings and proficiencies. When they had financial or practical needs, she helped them in those areas too. She would laugh with the teenagers' social media posts and cry with them when a pet died. She led with compassion and heart.

Unpacking this educator's multifaceted leadership strategies would require a book in itself. But I want to draw on some of Amber's methods to clarify relevant action points.

Ultimately, an exploration of authority must advance beyond theories and move into practical application. Our ideas have to work in the real world.

Based on exchanges with this educator and other influencers, I've highlighted *seven leadership mechanics*. This list isn't exhaustive, but I feel that it provides a useful place to expand our discussion.

Leaders *perceive, initiate, fund, disrupt, empower, protect,* and *inspire*. Let's unpack what each of these means.

1. LEADERS PERCEIVE

The first point I'd like to explore in the seven leadership mechanics is *vision*. Influencers without a wide-angle lens have a tough time getting their organization off the ground. Reflecting on the importance of this, Solomon declared: "Where there is no vision, the people perish" (Proverbs 29:18 KJV).

This passage isn't attaching vision to a leader's personal preferences or selfish ambitions. Vision has little to do with the interior world of an individual. Instead, it draws on a deeper awareness that transcends everyday affairs. Vision is rooted in the eternal destinies of nations, cities, and enterprises.

When individuals can't envision the greater purposes, it accelerates destruction. Another translation renders the sentiment this way: "Where there is no revelation, people cast off restraint." Societies need leaders who can help them see the loftier purposes.

Vision is the overriding concern. Elsewhere in Scripture, God revealed the following to the prophet Habakkuk: "Write down the vision and clearly inscribe it on tablets, so that a herald may run with it" (Habakkuk 2:2 CSB).

God wanted to clarify the unfolding revelation so that the entire community could implement it. If they wrote it down, anyone could execute it. The vision would become a matter of public record and a basis for communal action.

We need a duplicable mandate for long-term growth. If others cannot echo it, it will not be engrained in the tribe. Everybody needs to know where they are going.

Part of the gift-mix of a leader is to see the world from a higher plane. They can anticipate what the future holds and disclose it in a way that others can recognize. Those who can't see can't lead.

THE TWO SPIES

In preparation for Israel entering the promised land, Moses sent twelve men to spy out the land. Ten of them let obstacles distract them. They couldn't see beyond the giants or walled cities. Yet two of the spies, Joshua and Caleb, sidestepped the entanglements and pointed to a marvelous opportunity.

> Caleb tried to quiet the people as they stood before Moses. "Let's go at once to take the land," he said. "We can certainly conquer it!" (Numbers 13:30 NLT).

While most can only see obstacles, strategic leaders uncover *opportunities*. Like Joshua and Caleb, they sense where the community should be and believe that triumph will come.

Effective leaders highlight the future. They're burdened with taking people into an unexplored realm waiting to be actualized. They see beyond the shadows.

People tend to listen to leaders who take them into a hopeful tomorrow. They recognize that an *optimistic future* is better than a *bitter past*. Whoever owns the future owns the hearts of the people. Effective leaders set their eyes on what lays ahead.

A God-inspired vision enables individuals to take up a cause greater than themselves. Honestly, most followers will not get behind an *ordinary* endeavor. If it isn't remarkable, they won't take action.

The reason some leaders grapple with recruitment and monetary support is because of what they're offering. If the cause isn't substantial, the people won't respond.

Crowds tend to ignore what's common. But when they find a worthwhile cause, individuals become captivated. Whole communities will want to embrace a compelling vision.

KANSAS CITY ROYALS

In 2015, the Kansas City Royals baseball team won their first World Series Championship in nearly thirty years. The whole metro area, where I live, was ecstatic about this victory.

When the homecoming parade was planned on November 3, 2015, almost a million people went downtown. The bathrooms, sidewalks, and restaurants couldn't handle the crowds. People at Union Station could barely move because of the throngs of spectators.

Though conditions were miserable, the fans really didn't mind. You couldn't keep them away. Many skipped work and went without food. Some even soiled their clothing because they found nowhere to use the restroom. Most didn't care. Their team had won the championship, and fans were thrilled to have an opportunity to celebrate with the ball team.

People won't just watch television when an amazing event is happening in their city. When the extraordinary is underway, they will go the extra mile. Individuals have no trouble pouring onto the streets for political protests or raising their voices at critical moments. Most love being a part of a world-changing movement.

TOMS SHOES

The significance of a cause doesn't only apply to sports teams or a local church but also applies in business.

Over a decade ago, Blake Mycoskie felt the burden of providing shoes for disadvantaged children in the third world. However, instead of starting a charity, he decided to launch a for-profit business venture.

Whenever his company, *TOMS*, sells shoes, they give a pair to an impoverished child. Mycoskie's rallying cause, "One for one," is one of the reasons that his company became a runaway success.

People not only liked the comfort and style of TOMS shoes, but they also loved the idea of making a difference in the world.

When individuals believe in a cause, they don't mind supporting it with their wallets. Money always follows vision.

TOGGLING BETWEEN THE PRESENT AND FUTURE

Those with a calling and a solid grasp of the mission see what's ahead. As Tod Bolsinger brilliantly proclaims, whoever "takes personal responsibility to live in the new future in a transformative way in relationship to the others in the system is the leader."[1] Foresight within a community makes a difference.

But a vision-caster isn't solely concerned with the future. They're also embedded in the *here-and-now*. There's no getting around it; leaders must accurately interpret contemporary morés. *Vision* has as much to do with the *present* as it does with the *future*.

Peering ahead is crucial, but leaders must also be faithful with what's already in their hands. They cannot stand outside pre-existing relationships and organizational structures—that doesn't work. Prophets, scholars, and consultants can kick down the scaffolding, but ground level leaders can't. For better or worse, those in charge must learn how to operate *inside the system* and how to be more creative on a smaller canvas.

Moving forward, the *present-future* leader learns to make 360-degree assessments. They see ahead as well as behind. They are willing to ask some of the following questions:

- Who are we?
- What do we do?
- Why do we do it?
- How do we do it?

In order to advance, we must have a solid grasp of where we currently are. Bolsinger said, "No one is going to follow you off the map unless they trust you on the map."[2] A leader needs to inspire confidence in what people can see so individuals are willing to follow them in what cannot be seen.

WHAT NEHEMIAH SAW

Nehemiah, in the Old Testament, didn't speculate about reconstructing Jerusalem until he first laid eyes on the ruins. He had received reports, but he wanted a first-hand assessment in order to make decisions about how to move forward. He marked his vision within the context of on-the-ground necessities. The ability to solve problems depends on an appropriate analysis. Nehemiah said,

> The city where my ancestors are buried is in ruins, and the gates have been destroyed by fire. The king asked, "Well, how can I help you?" With a prayer to the God of heaven, I replied, "If it please the king, and if you are pleased with me, your servant, send me to Judah to rebuild the city where my ancestors are buried." The king, with the queen sitting beside him, asked, "How long will you be gone? When will you return?" After I told him how long I would be gone, the king agreed to my request. (Nehemiah 3b-6 NLT)

Leaders invariably have a *bias for action*. In many ways, this is an asset. However, they must accurately evaluate the situation. Wrong judgments transpire whenever there's a skewed perspective. Those on the front lines need to press in to see the whole picture before they act.

The forerunners should ask some of the following questions:

- What's going on behind the scenes?
- Who's making power plays?
- Is anyone lying or holding back details?
- How do we get things to the irreducible core?

These were the kinds of questions that Nehemiah had to wrestle with. Although leaders visualize what's *ahead*, they also ground their actions in *present-day realities*. They peer beyond the horizon, but their feet are firmly planted in the prevailing culture.

Understanding two realms at once is vital. World-changers might look to the *future*, but they live in the *now*.

IPHONE

Steve Jobs, the late CEO and visionary behind the Apple Corporation, introduced the iPhone on January 9, 2007. In this widely watched presentation, he opened with what is and pivoted to what could be.

Jobs reminded his audience how rudimentary cellphones were. Most devices could only call or receive text messages. The most expensive units had tiny screens, spotty internet access, and cumbersome keyboards.

After identifying where the world of technology stood, Jobs pulled out the state-of-the-art iPhone—wowing the audience with a large screen, intuitive interface, and built-in camera. Suddenly, the future broke into the present.

Jobs' innovative device was strategically framed against the shortcomings of contemporary technology. No matter how forward-leaning a product is, it only makes sense from a present-day context. By understanding what *is*, one can explain what *could be*.

VISION IS NOT THE SAME AS FUTURISM

Vision isn't a euphemism for futurism or playing around with novelties. Sometimes people think that they're leaders when they're merely tinkerers and curiosity seekers. Being *avant-garde* might make you "cool," but it doesn't make you a transformative force.

Not long ago, I received a phone call from an out-of-town friend. As we discussed innovation, Zack asked if I had read any articles in *Wired Magazine*, piquing my interest.

Creativity and the revolutionary usage of technology have fascinated him for years. This entrepreneur continually yearned to capture the zeitgeist of the age. Although I admired Zack's curiosity, he's often tangential. While enthralled with the stars in the sky, one might ignore the beauty lying in the dirt.

I reminded my friend that the old pathways deserve a second look. Sometimes progress comes by returning to the fundamentals.

Visionary leaders should learn how to navigate transitions well and find ways to advance into the future. But the way forward is seldom a straight line. The prophet Jeremiah proclaimed: "Ask for the old paths, where the good way is, and walk in it. Then you will find rest for your souls" (Jeremiah 6:16 NKJV).

Visionary leaders press into tomorrow, but that doesn't mean that their solutions are necessarily drawn from cutting-edge developments. Occasionally, the best action is to reconfigure an outmoded idea.

Visionary leaders think *anachronistically*—they envision realities outside the constraints of time. Leaders reach for the best answers, irrespective of their origin or length of use.

THE RESURGENCE OF RECORD ALBUMS

In the early 2000s, music companies watched as their sizable profits disappeared. Inexpensive digital downloads didn't produce the same returns on investment that cassettes and CDs had.

Around 2007, an executive noticed a spike in record sales. Although the format had mostly been phased out in the late 80s, a few new releases still came out as vinyl. This analyst discovered that consumers were buying new records and the used market was expanding. Popular older albums that had been going for a few dollars were now selling for $200 in resale shops.

The broad access and convenience of digital downloads appealed to most twenty-first century buyers. But a segment of the customer base did not want this format. For them, music was no longer tangible.

Superfans and audiophiles loved the artwork and liner notes

inside the older records. They also believed that the warm, analog sound was superior to the streaming services' compressed digital formats.

Music executives understood that the repackaging of dated concepts can lead to a marketplace resurgence. Retro items capture trendsetters' attention. This is precisely what happened with record albums around 2008.

Companies began packaging new vinyl recordings with multi-color booklets, copious liner notes, and priced as high as forty dollars. These records essentially thumbed their noses at digital formats, and the customers loved it.

By mid-2020, the old format outsold CDs in the United States for the first time since the 1980s.[3] Record sales could not offset all the monetary losses, but they did ease some of the tension. This development shows that under the right conditions, what's old can become new again.

Visionaries understand the path forward is sometimes identified by moving backward. Modern-day answers are occasionally found in yesterday's questions. Leaders must learn to see the world through various facets. While it defies logic to some extent, a reapplication of the past could transform how we see the present.

STAR WARS

George Lucas was an innovator, as we can see from his Star Wars film franchise. In his second trilogy of films—*The Phantom Menace* (1999), *The Attack of the Clones* (2002), and *The Revenge of the Sith* (2005)—he placed his actors in front of a green screen and utilized computer simulations. He used this state-of-the-art idea to produce stunning cinematography.

The use of cutting-edge technology has advantages but comes with a downside as well. It was relatively painless for Lucas to make modifications in post-production, but actors went without tangibles: set pieces, costumes, weapons, or creatures. Sometimes Lucas forced the actors to perform on an empty set.

Many felt that this approach to filmmaking hindered the quality of Lucas's films. The acting was stiff, and the environments were artificial. Somehow the blood, sweat, and rust of the original *Star Wars* film had been lost.

When J. J. Abrams directed the next *Star Wars* film, *The Force Awakens* (2015), he went back to the old approach to filmmaking. He gave actors beautifully designed sets, physical models, and simulated weaponry they could physically engage with. Abrams combined digital cinematography with real outdoor sets, enabling the performers to interact with each other within space and time.

This expensive process took longer to produce. But when Abrams' film came out, many felt that it was a return to form. *Star Wars: The Force Awakens* made over two billion dollars and broke numerous box office records.

Returning to previous patterns is a means to navigate the future. Being forward-thinking does not require the *latest* and *greatest*. Leaders shouldn't be distracted by the cool factor or similar cheap gimmicks. Vision is about recognizing what's genuinely best for the organization. It's about seeing the big picture.

IN THE SHADOW OF WHAT IS AND WHAT IS TO COME

Visionary leaders help people gaze beyond the horizon. While these men and women focus attention on tomorrow, their messaging is rooted in the present-day. Not frightened by the shifting shadows, they toggle between *what is* and *what is to come*.

Every generation grapples with an underlying struggle. Wrestling with his apprehensions, poet and essayist T. S. Eliot wrote, "Between the motion and the act falls the shadow."[4]

Leaders will wrestle for answers in the fog of the already and the not yet.

2. LEADERS INITIATE

Leadership is not just about vision. In fact, seeing and relating mission is rarely enough to get an enterprise moving. Plenty of individuals can prognosticate and theorize about the direction of the organization. They recognize the problems and are smart analysts, but they're not necessarily leaders.

Many assume that leadership means the accurate interpretation of a crisis. This can be one aspect of governance, but it's never the entirety of it. Recognizing the peculiarities of a problem is useful, but that ability doesn't necessarily provide an actual resolution.

In many instances, a significant segment of the organization is already familiar with the problems. The fact that someone on top finally notices the disruption doesn't mean much. Honestly, those affected are less concerned with appraisals than they are with action.

A leader may not be the first to see an obstacle (or recognize a new opportunity). They may not understand the issues as well as someone else does. But authority isn't about absolute knowledge or even the technical know-how to fix matters. Leadership is the readiness to take action. It's about becoming a person who will lead the way forward. Authority is rooted in action.

THE WRIGHT BROTHERS

The science of aerodynamics captivated artist Leonardo DiVinci and other brilliant minds. They conducted experiments, making detailed sketches of bird wings. In the succeeding centuries, controversies raged about what it would take for a man to fly.

In the 1890s, enterprising bicycle makers Orville and Wilbur Wright decided to do what no one had accomplished—build a working motorized aircraft.

At this time, aviation was a fashionable subject with significant progress being made. But few of the tinkerers and analysts were prepared to go all in. The Wright brothers were different. They were happy to throw themselves completely into this undertaking. They climbed on top of gliders and crudely mechanized airplanes before they were ready to carry anyone. Despite numerous crashes and personal injuries, the bicyclists persisted.

Immersing themselves into every component of this dangerous mission, the Wright brothers ultimately prevailed. On December 17, 1903, the tinkerers accomplished history's first sustained flight on the outskirts of Kitty Hawk, North Carolina.

Orville and Wilbur drew upon the research, equations, and practical suggestions of others. Although they made a crude wind tunnel to test their glider prototypes and designed propellers, they never claimed to be experts. Their focus was on building a working model.

The Wright brothers weren't leaders because they had the best designs or data; they were leaders because they were the first to go up in the air.

THEODORE ROOSEVELT

After Theodore Roosevelt became President of the United States, he wasted little time governing. He stirred multitudes with passionate rhetoric and a trembling fist. Roosevelt learned to "speak softly and carry a big stick."[5]

In one of his biggest moves, Roosevelt informed Congress about the prospect of digging a canal across the isthmus of Panama. This fifty-one-mile shortcut would connect the Atlantic and Pacific Oceans in the middle of the Americas. Roosevelt insisted that no other work "undertaken on this continent is as of such consequence."[6]

The opportunities were obvious to forward thinkers. But the old guard wasn't so sure. Skeptical about financing this risky enterprise, Congress wanted more time to deliberate. After dragging their feet, the initiative fell out of the public consciousness.

The impassioned Roosevelt couldn't sit by while the project was stymied. He journeyed to Panama and had his picture taken behind the controls of a ninety-five-ton steam shovel. The President demonstrated to Americans what it looked like to dig a moat in the Panamanian jungle. Roosevelt personified the mission as only he could, and the story was carried in newspapers around the world.

Roosevelt's audacious move reignited the public imagination and applied pressure to sluggish politicians. Within a short time, tens of millions of dollars were stipulated for the project. Despite setbacks, the work continued, and by 1913, the Panama Canal opened.

Presidents prior to Roosevelt were content with diplomacy and symbolic gestures. But this lion of a man wasn't satisfied with incrementalism. Roosevelt triumphed over lethargy and inaction with an unrelenting, hands-on approach. He wasn't afraid to embody the changes that he hoped to see. It's little wonder that Roosevelt is called the first modern president.[7]

LEADERSHIP IS SEIZING OPPORTUNITY

The leader isn't necessarily the first to *see* an opportunity—they're the first to *seize* it. They compel people to take action about the problem. Leaders are initiators.

The pages of the Bible are saturated with narratives of trailblazers, individuals willing to go off the map and establish a new way. Here is a list of a few of them:

- Noah and his sons spent decades building a large boat when they never saw a drop of rain (Genesis 6:9-22).

- Abraham journeyed with his family to find a city that they had never seen (Genesis 12:1-7; Hebrews 11:10).
- Moses, under the leading of God, determined Israel would leave Egypt and labored to free his people (Exodus 4:18-13:22).
- David was willing to take on Goliath while the rest of Israel was reluctant to advance into battle (1 Samuel 17:1-54).
- David later boldly pressed in for the ark of covenant to be brought into Jerusalem at a significant personal cost (2 Samuel 6:1-18).
- Elijah was willing to declare there would be no rain and then live amid the famine (1 Kings 17:1-18:46).
- When Nehemiah heard that Jerusalem was destroyed, he prayed and asked the king for permission to rebuild the wall (Nehemiah 1:1-2:10).
- Upon arriving in the city, Nehemiah called the officials together and planned the construction project. Nehemiah then persuaded all of the people to join him in rebuilding (Nehemiah 2:11-7:3).
- When Obadiah learned that Queen Jezebel was going to kill one hundred prophets, he took the initiative to hide them in caves and provide food (1 Kings 18:4).
- Upon hearing of famine in Jerusalem, Paul organized an offering and persuaded Gentile Christians to contribute (Acts 11:27-30).

The ancient biblical communities had individuals who boldly advanced into the unknown. They zealously pushed into the purposes before them. These battle-hardened people willingly pressed on to the finish line.

Twenty-first century leaders must have a similar outlook. Those who hope to build a lasting legacy must be proactive, applying what is necessary to progress. They never back down from a difficult assignment. All they know is forward momentum.

Leaders are willing to wade into the waters and abandon the comfort of everything they know. They are relentless in advancement, ready to apprehend the prize.

JOSHUA CHAMBERLAIN AND THE CIVIL WAR

An initiator is not just a person in business, politics, or ministry People in other fields are proactive as well. For example, Joshua Chamberlain, a mild-mannered teacher from Bowdoin College in Maine, was burdened by the cause of freedom. He enlisted in the 20th Maine Infantry Regime during the initial years of the Civil War.

After minimal conflict, on the morning of July 2, 1863, the dynamics changed. Chamberlain's unit was strategically positioned at the end of the Union line on a small hill near Gettysburg, Pennsylvania.

As the last unit, they were assigned to hold off Confederate advances. If they failed, the South would turn in from behind and annihilate the Northern battalions. They didn't know it, but Chamberlain and his fellow soldiers were standing at the turning point of the war.

The Confederate army raced up the hill twice, and the 20th Maine fought them off on both occasions. This victory, however, came with an enormous price. With over half of the unit fallen, most of the Union officers were dead.

With Chamberlain now at the helm, he found himself in a desperate situation. He was ordered to hold the ground at all costs. If the 20th Maine pulled out, the South would advance. But with most of his unit dead and a shortage of ammunition, the North didn't have much hope for victory.

As the Confederates were assembling for another advance,

Chamberlain knew some of his men wanted to retreat. He had to make a quick decision. Facing an almost certain death, he ordered the men to fix their bayonets. Outnumbered and out-armed, Chamberlain was prepared to do what was required—sacrificially march into oblivion.

With a bayonet affixed to an empty gun, he hopped up and cried, "Charge!" The first one, he rushed over the line and down the rocky incline. At the sight of his courage, other soldiers fell into line behind him with a thunderous shout.

The Confederates were noticeably shaken. They concluded that the 20th Maine had gained reinforcements. Many threw down their rifles and simply surrendered. Chamberlain and his men managed to overtake a well-armed Southern Army twice their size.

This action halted the Confederate advance and permitted the Northern armies to triumph at Gettysburg—a battle that turned the tide of the war. The determination of one man changed a nation.

LEADERSHIP IS HARD WORK

Changing the world requires blood, sweat, and tears. Authentic leaders never recoil in the face of hard work. John C. Maxwell, the leadership specialist, likes to say, "The pessimist complains about the wind. The optimist expects it to change. The leader adjusts the sails." [8] Society needs less talk and more action. They want more doers.

Initiating projects is a part of humanity's original design. Not long after Adam was given his original mandate, he was instructed to *work*. Scripture reveals, "God took the man and put him in the Garden of Eden to work it and take care of it" (Genesis 2:15 NIV). Before sin entered the picture, humanity was already at work, stewarding and building.

In the New Testament, the apostle Paul was busy launching local churches and establishing mission fields. He reminded some of the leaders in the Corinthian church that he had "labored and toiled" and had "often gone without sleep" (2 Corinthians 11:24). Being in charge is never a cake walk.

Successful leaders are continually pushing for personal and organizational transformation. They understand that if you don't move forward, you'll be stuck in the past. If you aren't coming alive, you're probably dying.

Leaders are not afraid to initiate. They are willing to sacrificially advance in the most challenging seasons. They cannot walk away from their assignments. A real leader refuses to give up. They willingly fight all the way to the end.

3. LEADERS FUND

Leadership is not just about *vision* or *initiation* but is also about gathering the necessary resources. Leaders pull together what is required so that organizations can function.

Entrepreneurs recognize the importance of cultivating and educating investors. Without an infusion of venture capital, innovations cannot be brought to market. It's not just ideas, but fiscal leadership that births inventions.

Ideally, the startup leader is not merely forming a corporation that improves society; they're also enabling shareholders to receive a financial return. Individuals who invested in Google or YouTube, in their earliest inceptions, not only helped launch notable companies; they also saw an exponential return on their contributions.

Leaders proactively ask individuals to support their plans with a suitable financial investment. Money tends to follow vision and purpose.

UBER

In 2008, Travis Kalanick and Garrett Camp attended a technology conference in Paris but couldn't hail a cab. Frustrations about missing their appointment sparked the idea of Uber.

Kalanick imagined a tech-driven company that provided rapid-response, crowd-sourced car rides. Riders could be picked up and be on their way in a matter of minutes through a GPS enabled smartphone app.

The founders needed investors to take the company nationwide. In one of the first meetings with venture capitalists, the Uber team explained the opportunity to improve on taxi services and enrich investors in the process. The future could break into the present, and the individuals in the room were positioned to be catalysts for this needed change.

The Uber presenter explained, "People wait forty-five minutes for a taxi, and then the service cancels on you with minimal notice." He told them that the marketplace was demanding an easier and more reliable transport service, and Uber, with its digital strategies and crowd-sourced drivers, would fit the bill.[9]

Unsurprisingly, the investors found the company's vision compelling. Uber quickly raised over $1.25 million and made its Wall Street debut with a valuation of $80 billion. Seth Fiegerman writes

> Investors who participated in that first Uber funding round earned staggering financial returns, bragging rights within the industry and front row seats to the rise of a company that would go on to shake up transportation and labor markets around the world.[10]

Powerful ideas, ripe for marketplace expansion, will receive ample funding. Visionaries understand that if one doesn't buy a stake in tomorrow, they'll be left behind in yesterday. Every living thing either grows or dies.

The early investors in Uber became wealthy, but they also altered how individuals were being transported in the twenty-first century. Many were as excited about being on the cutting edge of technology as they were about increasing wealth. People want to be a part of creating change in society.

Money tends to follow interesting, well-articulated ideas. But innovations won't be funded if no one fights for them. When the mission of an enterprise is clear, contributions will come in. Compelling vision-casters pick up the needed resources so that operations can commence.

ALS AND THE ICE BUCKET CHALLENGE

Leaders aren't afraid to color outside the lines. They know that capital can come by unconventional means. To get the job done, an innovator might have to think multidimensionality.

For example, in 2014, Patrick Quinn, Peter Frates, and Anthony Senerchia, came up with a strategy to increase funding for the research of a rare neurodegenerative neuromuscular disorder. Amyotrophic lateral sclerosis (ALS), also known as Lou Gehrig's Disease, attacks motor functions. With this neurological disorder, people lose the capacity to speak, move, and breathe. This diagnosis is a death sentence.

Grants tend to go toward investigations of illnesses that affect a higher percentage of society—heart disease, cancer, and leukemia. So, with fewer than 20,000 ALS patients in the United States, funding wasn't as accessible.

To remedy this, Quinn, Frates, and Senerchia came up with the Ice Bucket Challenge. Supporters poured a bucket of ice water over their head, gave to an ALS charity, and challenged friends on social media to repeat this pattern. The chilly water running down their body was filmed and shared on social media.

This fundraising technique went viral, and over 17 million people posted videos online. A number of celebrities, including Oprah, Chris Pratt, Bill Gates, and former President George W. Bush, championed the cause. For a while, this became the number one trending topic in America.

In an effort to end amyotrophic lateral sclerosis, the Ice Bucket Challenge raised over $220 million. This money significantly boosted the development of pharmaceuticals and treatment regimens.[11] These results came from people sharing silly videos.

The ALS Association acknowledged that Quinn, Frates, and Senerchia's ice buckets "dramatically accelerated the fight against ALS, leading to new research discoveries, expanded care for people living with ALS, and significant investment from the government in ALS research."[12]

Money will come to those who find innovative ways to tell their story. Leaders are only limited by the constraints of their imaginations.

MARSHALING THE RESOURCES

Leaders have to be proactive in the area of finances. While some marketplace leaders have bristled at the idea of fundraising, I've encountered much worse from fellow ministers. More than one has told me, "I wasn't called to take up offerings or talk about money. I was called to preach the gospel."

An individual with legitimate authority will work to pull together resources. Papa is continuously concerned about paying the bills. They are responsible for the welfare and provision of the family. They won't just stand by when there is a need.

One leader told me, "I don't want to go there because of the negative associations with money." I get it. Everyone knows examples of financial abuse. Some televangelists have been swayed by ill-gotten wealth and exploited their positions of power. Likewise, greed in multinational corporations is legendary. Too many people are only about the bottom line. Yet the misdeeds of a few should not color everything else. God calls leaders to mobilize individuals in every aspect of the mission.

We cannot overlook finances or the acquisition of resources. These are as important as any other part of the process.

CHURCHES SHOULD THINK OUTSIDE THE BOX

Ministry leaders have to be responsible for the mission. Part of what God is calling ministry leaders to do is to think outside the box. Some funding streams might be accessed through innovative means. Thinking shouldn't be limited.

There's nothing wrong with receiving conventional offerings at church, but pastors can supplement this stream of income in other ways. James Murphy with the Episcopal Church Foundation writes,

> Churches must consider additional income streams beyond regular donations. Creative opportunities should be considered, such as installing cell phone towers inside church steeples or investigating rental opportunities.[13]

Congregations can also start day-cares or private schools and partner with for-profit enterprises. They don't have to limit their options as they did decades ago. They can explore other avenues.[14]

Twenty-first century leaders must seriously consider every available means. Some growth mechanisms on the periphery might have never been utilized. Think bigger.

GOD DOESN'T HATE MONEY

Sometimes Christians have a warped view of finances. Many of the misguided say: "Money is the root of all evil" (1 Timothy 6:10 KJV). This excerpt often distorts the original context. A fuller reading of the biblical text shows the following:

> For the love of money is a root of all kinds of evil. Some people, in their eagerness to get rich, have wandered away from the faith and caused themselves a lot of pain. (1 Timothy 6:10 ISV)

This Scripture isn't a repudiation of money but rather a warning about how to approach wealth. The Bible is not against people possessing gold; it's against gold possessing people. The Bible's underlying outlook shouldn't be distorted.

In another relevant Bible passage, the Lord makes a declaration about giving individuals "the ability to produce wealth" (Deuteronomy 8:18 ISV). In other words, God enables people, by his grace, to build, invest, and gather resources. Biblical covenants were often built on the idea of human increase and expansion. It's a mistake to overlook the implications of this verse.

In another passage, we can see God's intentions. After the global flood, God told Noah, "As long as the earth endures, there will be seedtime and harvest" (Genesis 8:22 ESV). The viability of *prosperity* is hardwired into creation itself. Those who understand the natural order will find increase.

To say that God is opposed to wealth and the acquisition of resources is ridiculous. That sentiment misses much of what undergirds the Word of God. The Lord made us to be enterprising and fruitful.

CAPITAL CAMPAIGNS IN THE BIBLE

The spiritual realm is not in conflict with the material, and God isn't dismissive of ethical fund-raising. In fact, several biblical passages demonstrate the importance of leaders gathering necessary resources. God unapologetically uses anointed men and women to pull together resources for the mission. Consider the following examples.

Moses, the notable patriarch and lawgiver, courageously stood up and took responsibility for gathering materials to erect the tabernacle.

> Then Moses said to the whole community of Israel, "This is what the Lord has commanded: Take a sacred offering for the Lord. Let those with generous hearts present the following gifts to the Lord: gold, silver, and bronze; blue, purple, and scarlet thread; fine linen and goat hair for cloth; tanned ram skins and fine goatskin leather; acacia wood; olive oil for the lamps; spices for the anointing oil and the fragrant incense; onyx stones, and other gemstones to be set in the ephod and the priest's chest piece." (Exodus 35:4-9 NLT)

What's impressive about this story is that Moses was so fruitful in his undertaking that he had to ask the families to stop giving. Can you imagine gathering too many resources?

Let's look at another Old Testament figure, King David. Although he wasn't released to erect the temple of the Lord, he took it upon himself to collect all that was required for its construction. David said:

> I have worked hard to provide materials for building the Temple of the Lord—nearly 4,000 tons of gold, 40,000 tons of silver, and so much iron and bronze that it cannot be weighed. I have also gathered timber and stone for the walls, though you may need to

> add more. You have a large number of skilled stonemasons and carpenters and craftsmen of every kind. You have expert goldsmiths and silversmiths and workers of bronze and iron. Now begin the work, and may the Lord be with you! (1 Chronicles 22:14-16 NLT)

David received many of the materials before he died, understanding that one of his greatest legacies would be in the offering that he raised for Solomon. Leadership can be facilitated simply by gathering and releasing resources for the next generation.

Stories about leaders willing to pull together what's needed aren't just an Old Testament reality. In the New Testament, the apostle Paul also took it upon himself to collect funds to help the church in Jerusalem. Paul writes

> I am pleased to inform you that the believers of Macedonia and Greece have made a generous contribution for the poor among the holy believers in Jerusalem. They were thrilled to have an opportunity to give back to the believers in Jerusalem. For indeed, they are deeply grateful for them and feel indebted because they brought them the gospel. Since the ethnic multitudes have shared in the spiritual wealth of the Jewish people, it is only right that the non-Jewish people share their material wealth with them. So, when I have completed this act of worship and safely delivered the offering to them in Jerusalem, I will set out for Spain and visit you on my way there (Romans 15:26-28 TPT).

The apostle was letting us know that generosity was a display of unity for the churches as well as a tangible way to help the Jerusalem assembly experiencing setbacks at that time. Pulling together finances accomplishes several things at once.

Paul prioritized investing in the church's needs, teaching others to follow these same values. Every leader must understand the truth that money and mission go hand in hand.

BELIEVE IN THE MISSION

Leaders need to learn how to embrace proper mindsets about money. Too many distorted ideals keep organizations from advancing. A mindset rooted in lack will restrict growth. Funding is not just the concern of benefactors; it is also the burden of visionaries. If no one is responsible, the work won't be completed.

Discussing money is never easy, but strategic leaders don't hesitate to ask individuals to stand behind the enterprise. If one doesn't believe in a cause enough to ask for contributions, the mission might not be worthwhile. If the leader doesn't believe in it, then neither do I.

4. LEADERS DISRUPT

Influential leaders don't just gather resources; they also disrupt environments. Those with authority are willing to start over from scratch. They're more burdened with the *mission* than the *methods*.

Culture is embedded in every enterprise. These priorities color all aspects of the company: the attitudes, tone, and processes that undergird the group activities.

When I'm talking about culture, what I mean is the operating system, or as one of my friends explained, "The unseen water that the fish swim in." Culture is not *what* but *how*, the forms and structures brandished by an enterprise.

We can celebrate aspects of every organizational culture but should reconsider other parts—particularly when they inhibit the purposes of the venture.

Most enterprises were established on mission. The team hobbled together a way to accomplish tasks. The practical processes had no significant attachments. But over time, methods can become mere form and habits.

Adam Grant, a researcher at Wharton, points out that as an

organization gains more expertise and experience, it becomes more entrenched in a particular way of viewing the world." Whenever "we gain knowledge about a domain, we become prisoners of our prototypes."[15]

A maturing organization will often become more concerned with how they operate than with what they're producing. Over time, the survival of the organization "becomes the prevailing vision, and the mission becomes about sustaining the method."[16] Many aging organizations are caught up in mission drift.

Sometimes a leader needs to poke the bear, re-examining the boundaries of the organization. They need to scrutinize cultures if the enterprise wants to continue in the ideals that it was founded on. Leadership is a willingness to put mission before the structures and traditions of the institution.

GOOGLE

Decades ago, companies in the tech industry were indistinguishable from corporations in other sectors. Employees put on suits and worked nine-to-five. Introverted software engineers were required to collaborate with others. No one in that era could have worked from home.

When Larry Page and Sergey Brin launched Google in 1998, they disrupted many older paradigms. The founders, for example, introduced casual dress, flex-time, and telecommuting. That wasn't all.

One of Page's and Brin's most unusual innovations was the 20%-time policy. Google employees were encouraged to allocate one-fifth of their time (one day a week) pursuing ideas outside their ordinary responsibilities. These side efforts produced Gmail, Google News, and AdSense, producing billions in revenue.

At Google, promotions and raises didn't just go to management. The board found ways to compensate employees with technological skills. They valued every component of the business.

In order for this strategy to work, Page and Brin had to trust their employees and be willing to manage operations differently. Page and Brin ultimately reconfigured the ecosystem of their tech offices, transforming business culture.

Page and Brin theorized that these approaches would unleash creativity and productivity. Against a myriad of naysayers, they were proven right.

Google became a maverick company, upsetting much of what had governed the marketplace for a century. With their modern approach to operations and profits, other businesses paid close attention. The business sector would never be the same after Google disrupted the marketplace.

JOHN WESLEY

Another notable disruptor was John Wesley, an eighteenth-century revivalist. He established a religious society within the Church of England called Methodism.

Anglicans often became enmeshed in British politics and focused on gaining affluence. Officials were consumed with safeguarding the boundaries of English society and had little room for conversions, missions, or spiritual revival.

The Anglican bishops tolerated Wesley's rag-tag society but never championed it. To consecrate his evangelists, Wesley needed the blessing of the bishops. But the religious bureaucrats were inclined to disregard the society's needs. They thought that the Methodists were too noisy and bothersome.

The Methodists found a work around until they received an opportunity to send ministers to the United States. In the post-Revolutionary era, Americans wanted no associations with the Anglican Church or its so-called societies.

For the Methodist missionaries to thrive in this environment, Wesley needed to break with the old paradigms. Operating outside the Anglican bishop's jurisdiction, Wesley laid hands on these men himself and released them for the mission.

This procedure permitted a newly independent Methodist Church to gain a foothold in the United States. Abandoning the Anglican Church's politics and social sensibilities, young preachers effectively spread the fires of revival.

Wesley was prepared to upend his lifelong religious culture for the sake of mission. Even so, Anglican clerics and his old classmates from Oxford University criticized him for this. Still, this decision positively transformed millions of lives.[17]

As John Wesley broke with the old paradigms, a whole new way of experiencing Christian worship emerged. Upsetting the apple cart sometimes enables new expressions to take root.

CHALLENGING THE CULTURE

The easiest thing that a leader can do is maintain the *status quo*. The old tried-and-true methods rarely cause trouble. A lot of so-called leaders are comfortable fitting into an old mold. One told me, "I think it's best to keep doing what we've been doing. What got us here is good enough."

I understand the pressure to stay with older approaches. Everyone is accustomed to that. But sometimes, the entrenched patterns undermine the work. What may have worked years ago might not work anymore.

Many corporations are declining across the United States because no one has stood up to defy the culture or outdated industry practices.

Virtually every newspaper is going bankrupt in the opening decades of the twenty-first century. The owners mistakenly thought they were in the paper, ink, and trucking business rather than in the news business. They kept investing in old supply chains and irrelevant mechanisms.

The multi-billion-dollar music industry is also experiencing financial ruin because the executives ignored the internet's rise. The business pioneers never dreamed consumers would listen to streams online and would stop purchasing recorded music. Currently, more than half of the music industry's revenues come from live music.[18] The industry has shifted.

In major cities, young adults are no longer buying automobiles. In most cases, they would rather bicycle or walk. When I visited Michigan Avenue in Chicago, I noticed massive bike garages. Who in the auto industry is grappling with the fact that America is different from what it was in 1985? The kids don't want sedans.

All of these institutions needed someone to confront their faded business models. Anyone paying attention could see what was looming. For decades, marketplaces have been moving in this direction.

Companies desperately needed leaders to challenge the culture of their enterprises. But the disruptors were habitually silenced. Those who wanted to break with the status quo were accused of "crying wolf" or of drawing attention to themselves. Most of the board members were too close to retirement or too entrenched in pre-existing structures to pay attention.

Strategic leaders are not afraid to discard what no longer works. They are not locked into a particular technique or style. These men and women are willing to confront their organization's stagnant culture and design something new and relevant.

FACING DISRUPTIONS HEAD-ON

I foresee, within a few years, people will not leave their house very often. Telecommuting—individuals working from their living room

—was already increasing before the coronavirus pandemic. It has expanded even further since.

Business leaders are increasingly pivoting away from the office. Surveys reveal that many firms "intend to permanently shift some of their jobs off-site."[19] More than 47 percent of CEOs "say they intend to allow full-time remote work going forward."[20]

Virtually everything is being re-centered in the home. As Scott Galloway observes,

> Amazon, of course, took the store and dispersed it to our front door. Netflix took the movie theater and put it in our living room. We're going to see this dispersion across other industries, including healthcare.[21]

With Facetime, Zoom, and other video applications, individuals can have face-to-face conversations with out-of-town colleagues online. Fareed Zakaria, writes,

> When I was in college, a three-minute call to my mother in India was so expensive that I had to budget the call and watch the clock. Today my daughter can spend five hours on Face-Time with a friend in Singapore and it costs nothing.[22]

The ability to ship food and other merchandise also becomes more cost-efficient every year. I'm a member of Amazon Prime. I can order a paperback book with a single click and be reading it in two days. DoorDash can bring my household meals from tasty local restaurants ten minutes after they're prepared. With so much available online, brick-and-mortar shops are less necessary than they used to be.

In the years ahead, people will only leave home for work, medical needs, or entertainment. As the spheres of interaction are reconfigured, leaders will have to pivot with them. The future of our enterprises depends on grappling with what's happening in the kitchen.

CHURCH UPHEAVALS

Right now, few are considering what's transpiring in local churches. Many pastors are entangled in peripheral issues and are out of touch with the most vital questions and needs of the hour. Issues of identity and engagement continue to shape the dialogue.

Unsurprisingly, the coronavirus pandemic has amplified underlying problems and forced new dialogues among believers. Episcopal Bishop Jeffery D. Lee observes,

> Epidemics are the great accelerators—or amplifiers—of realities, trends, flaws, and strengths in cultures and societies across the world. With breathtaking speed, that reality has now become undeniable in the church. The trends of institutional decline—particularly evinced by reductions in worship attendance, financial support, and formal affiliation—are accelerating and/or morphing quickly in this time of pandemic.[23]

Prior to COVID-19, believers were already engaging with church through the internet, watching sermon excepts, and sharing memes. Although ministry leaders were hesitant to accept that God could move through a screen, the masses readily embraced it.[24] Families were already comfortable merging digital and physical experiences. Many didn't "see a separation between real life and digital life. It's just life."[25]

Astoundingly, prior to the pandemic, "more than 250,000 congregations had never had a digital presence of any kind."[26] The lockdowns and loss of access to members naturally became a catalyst for new online engagement. Churches readily embraced video streams and classes on Zoom. Thom Rainer notes,

> The same digital tools that were being used before are still being used today, but now those tools are being used more vigorously and enthusiastically. What has changed is the perspective of the digital world among church leaders and members.[27]

Ministry leaders are certainly paying attention to digital tools more than ever before. They have seen the handwriting on the wall.

THE NEW NORMAL

Many church leaders don't recognize "COVID-19 is a shot across the bow of cultural Christianity."[28] They imagine everything will return to normal after the pandemic abates, but that's not likely. Pre-coronavirus and post-coronavirus aren't the same. Church members are not as inclined to go back to how things were.

In the past, leaders gauged congregational health by the number of times people came to the facility for worship services. But those metrics may have to be reconsidered.

One devout church attender shared the following thoughts on Facebook with Thom Rainer after being in lockdown for a few weeks:

> I have been going to church for so many years I don't even know how long it's been. It was what I was supposed to do. Now I sleep in on Sunday, and I may or may not watch the *Facebook* service. I really like this new schedule. I am really not sure I want to go back to church like I used to. It's a big hassle.[29]

Susan is not an outlier. According to a recent survey by the Barna Group, many Christians are contemplating a hybrid-church experience—digital and in-person. Only 41 percent of Gen Z (1996–present), 42 percent of millennials (1981–1995), and 47 percent of Gen X (1965–1980) want to return exclusively to in-person worship. That means that as many as 53 percent of Christians under fifty-five don't plan to be in the building as often.[30]

Among Baby Boomers, the number that plans to return to in-person worship is 71 percent. While this is a higher percentage than other age groups, it still means that 29 percent of the oldest and most-established church members don't want the physical church experience to be their primary point of engagement.[31]

While these numbers undoubtedly reflect the insanity of this season and will change with the passing of time, many families will still lean into digital connections. Web-based engagement is inevitable.

I like to ask questions, so I talked to Jessica, a twenty-eight-year-old single mom. I wanted feedback from a millennial on the significance of online church engagement. She told me the following:

> People like to do online church because they don't have to dress up, have awkward interactions, or commute to a building across town. Individuals need less fuss in their lives and want their faith experiences to be more uplifting.

Though serious about her faith, Jessica was ambivalent about in-person gatherings. She wasn't bothered in the least about being unorthodox. Like Thom Rainer's Facebook friend, she felt like a typical Sunday morning service was "a big hassle" for her family. She said, "What works for one might not work as readily for another." Church leaders might not agree with her sentiment, but it probably represents the views of millions of believers.

BOTH/AND

None of this is easy. Wise elders will argue that Christians still need to meet together and encounter *authentic community*. I agree.

Christ-followers do need to keep gathering face-to-face. The writer of Hebrews elaborates on this unmistakable biblical paradigm. "Let us not neglect our meeting together, as some people do" (Hebrews 10:25 NLT). Authentic believers will continue to gather because the church is inherently communal. What we do together will always be greater than what we do alone.

But if our society keeps moving along its present trajectory, newcomers will be less open to physical engagement. Unmindful of spiritual benefits or what the Bible says, they're motivated by their own sensibilities. People never ask stakeholders for permission to change. They just do it.

Is our faith big enough to engage people in the virtual world?[32] I hope so. Leaders must be willing to go where people are. People are struggling with their faith and desire digital technologies that "deepen our spiritual experience rather than deteriorate it."[33]

Leaders need to meet people where they are before they can persuade them to change. God's mission is more about investing in people than it is about a functioning in a particular locale.

In the days to come, leaders will have to connect with individuals through diverse avenues, showing them the value of face-to-face engagements. Fortunately, the increase of technology will amplify the desire for human connection. With so much online, people will have an insatiable hunger for personal interactions. They will want to experience a human connection in the midst of a digital wasteland.

However you frame it, Christian leaders will need to pivot, experiment, and energetically respond in a changing cultural context. The readjustments aren't about technology but about the way humans relate. Future ministry will not be *either/or* but *both/and.*

EXPERIENCES, RELATIONSHIPS, AND APPLICABLE CONTENT

As I said, in this disruptive era, church leaders are struggling. They are discovering that most of the go-to methods are no longer working. With a myriad of obstacles, ministers are forced to become trailblazers—journeying beyond the borders of the old maps.

No one has all the answers, and action points can be a matter of debate. But I'm convinced that a focus on the following elements could position a local church for greater advancement:

- Experiences
- Relationships
- Applicable Content

By experiences, I'm referring to what congregants encounter during a worship service, such as the lighting, sound, and atmosphere of the room. But it also refers to dynamic spiritual engagements. Many are looking for moments of transcendence. They want personal, emotional, and genuine environments. Potent in-person experiences can't be easily duplicated online.

It's also tough to establish meaningful relationships on the internet. So congregations should work on building environments for interaction, helping people connect. Individuals still need friends, and they might not find great ones online.

Churches accentuate the role of preaching, but the messaging is seldom directed toward felt needs. Pastors enjoy theology and high-level studies, but members rarely pursue these topics. Sermons should unveil the glory of heaven, but they also should help individuals with their day-to-day lives. Relevant churches in the future will highlight applicable content in their online and in-person messaging. People want to hear things that they can put into practice in their day-to-day lives.

Christian leaders who emphasize experiences, relationships, and applicable content will continue to influence emerging generations. Fellowships, focusing in this direction, will continue to increase in their in-person gatherings, because families will go out of their way to access this. They will eagerly seek personalized, interactive environments with relevant elements.

Christian leaders have to be mindful about what's ahead. If not, they will miss many opportunities.

LEADERS ARE CULTURE MAKERS

Society needs authorities who will challenge older environments and facilitate necessary changes. If a leader doesn't press into the future, they will find their organization on the losing end of societal shifts.

The leader who ignores this will be like a man selling pagers at a mall kiosk or a newspaper trying to sell classified advertising. The business models of previous eras don't work anymore. A leader can never forget that families are too busy to notice what is irrelevant. Out of sight is out of mind.

Terrified of rocking the boat, many are reluctant to confront the status quo. If you plan to be a leader, you will need to take necessary risks. A change agent should anticipate disruptions.

Leaders are culture makers. They transform the environments and the marketplaces surrounding them. You must be willing to engage in this so that your influence can go as far as possible.

5. LEADERS EMPOWER

We have discussed vision, initiation, resourcing, and culture. Now I want to point out another component: the willingness of a leader to *empower others*.

Sometimes established authorities are hesitant about this. According to investigations by Ed Stetzer and other analysts, a major impediment for churches is the lack of leadership development.[34]

Several pastors have told me they have no one to invest in. But they don't appear to be prospecting for others. Surely, individuals in their fellowship have potential, even if they're rough around the edges. These folks are available although a leader might have to look for them.

Moses had to grapple with this problem in his day. His father-in-law Jethro observed what was occurring. He said, "What you are doing is not good." He encouraged Moses to hand off some of his duties to other competent people.

> The next day, Moses took his seat to hear the people's disputes against each other. They waited before him from morning till evening. When Moses' father-in-law saw all that Moses was doing for the people, he asked, "What are you really accomplishing here? Why are you trying to do all this alone while everyone stands around you from morning till evening?" Moses replied, "Because the people come to me to get a ruling from God. When a dispute arises, they come to me, and I am the one who settles the case between the quarreling parties. I inform the people of God's decrees and give them his instructions." "This is not good!" Moses' father-in-law exclaimed. (Exodus 18:13-17 NLT)

Jethro's wisdom needs to be carried into the present day. Much of what we're doing is still not good. Established leaders need to open up a few more seats at the table.

Many high level authorities "design things for people, rather than design with them."[35] Building on the future is not merely sharing a few areas of responsibility or involving younger leaders in operations. While there are advantages to this, the next generation needs a strategic investment.

One of the most significant tasks for an established leader is to champion those who are just emerging.

WALT DISNEY

Institutions typically excel during the lifespan of the founder. But after he or she passes from the scene, the corporation stagnates. The Walt Disney Company is a rare exception. The corporation is more vital now than it was when Walt was alive.

Walt Disney, the American icon, became famous through his animated short *Steamboat Willie* (1928), the first cartoon with synchronized sound. He introduced the affable Mickey Mouse to the world. Disney went on to produce *Snow White and the Seven Dwarfs* (1938), *Pinocchio* (1940), *Cinderella* (1950), and other beloved classics.

Walt Disney built his company on collaborative leadership. His feature-length animated movies required hundreds of individuals focusing on details and continuity. Studio photos from the 1930s and '40s show Walt seated around the table with animators. While making the final decisions, he valued the input of others.

Walt genuinely wanted his company to break out of the box, and he loved to hear creative ideas. A few of the innovators close to him were deemed "imagineers" because they were able to combine engineering with the spark of imagination.

After Walt Disney died in 1966, the next generation advanced his vision. They went on to construct the Walt Disney World theme park (1971) and EPCOT—Experimental Prototype Community of Tomorrow (1982). Both enterprises were drawn from Walt's sketchbook, but they took his vision a step further.

That passion continues. The Walt Disney Company continues to lead on multiple fronts. Their phenomenal business acquisitions —*Star Wars, Marvel, Muppets, Simpsons,* Twentieth Century Fox— have produced considerable profits and transformed the modern entertainment industry.

Over the decades, the company also maintained the culture of creative advancements. The science fiction film *TRON* (1982) opened up visual effects in filmmaking. The Pixar division was praised for a heartfelt return to storytelling and animation practices. The corporation also broke ground with the Disney+ app, monetizing a treasure trove of television and films from their vaults. This direct-to-consumer platform will impact future film releases and position Disney to expand even further.

The Walt Disney Company has continued to prosper, even after the death of the founder. The creator of *Mickey Mouse* released a ground-breaking vision to the next generation, and they ran with it. Every now and then, the sons outpace the father.

APPLE

As I said, many ground-breaking companies lose their way after their founder's death. Influential brands get watered down. The Apple Corporation is an illustration of this. After co-founder Steve Jobs died in 2011, the company slowly lost its innovative spark.

Reflecting on this dilemma, Laura Sydell, a journalist with *National Public Radio* writes,

> Both Apple fans and analysts who follow the company are beginning to wonder whether Apple has lost its mojo . . . the iMac, the iPod, the iPhone, the iPad . . . All those innovations happened when Steve

> Jobs, Apple's co-founder, was running the company . . . Some former employees say a cultural shift occurred at Apple after Jobs died.[36]

For decades, *Apple*'s identity marker was innovation. From 1997–2002, their chief ad campaigns said, "Think Different,"[37] and the company delivered on that slogan. One tech insider quipped, "It's daunting to think about the number of products Apple created that have transformed how most people use technology."[38]

Disclosing his outlook, Steve Jobs declared,

> Some people say give the customers what they want, but that's not my approach. Our job is to figure out what they're going to want before they do. I think Henry Ford once said, "If I'd ask customers what they wanted, they would've told me a faster horse." People don't know what they want until you show it to them. That's why I never rely on market research. Our task is to read things that are not yet on the page.[39]

For Apple "to maintain its leadership" in the tech industry, Jobs felt the company "would need to repeat this strategy of innovating its way to success."[40] He declared in his commencement speech at Stanford University, "Innovation distinguishes between a leader and a follower."[41]

Under Jobs's leadership, Apple was on the cutting edge, but now most "innovation is coming from other companies."[42] Devoted customers are fortunate to get enhanced speed and a sharper camera on their new iPhones.[43]

Tim Cook, Jobs's successor, is capable but doesn't have the same drive. Bob Burrough, a collaborator on the development of the iPhone, acknowledges that "the culture at Apple changed when Tim Cook took over."[44]

Apparently, Jobs didn't ignite passion in Cook or any of the second-generation team. No one was encouraged to color outside the lines. Without disrupters, Apple has grown stagnant. Scott Galloway points out that

> Innovation is dangerous and unpredictable. It changes market dynamics and creates opportunities for nimble new players to steal shares from established players. None of that is attractive to an entrenched market leader.[45]

Galloway exposes what may have happened to Apple. Insiders in the company see less of an upside in implementing cutting-edge developments. A mistake could result in significant quarterly losses, angering the shareholders. Incremental change guarantees a better return on the investment in the short term.

A decade after Job's death, Apple is still making loads of money—more than $1 trillion dollars in a recent fiscal year. But they aren't turning many heads.

While it may be risky, passion and innovation must be cultivated in the next generation. Emerging leaders need to be given the freedom to experiment and build. Many wonderful things can be stewarded if a father works with his sons and daughters.

KATHRYN KUHLMAN FOUNDATION

Within enterprises, succession is often confusing or non-existent. Most founders see the discussion of a future without them as a mechanism for their own demise. One aging owner gruffly exclaimed, "Why should I be thinking about what's coming after me while I'm still here? There will be time enough for that later on."

Hesitations about succession are particularly noticeable in large religious organizations. Whenever the head of a national ministry dies, questions abound as to who will take the reins. The Kathryn Kuhlman Foundation was one example of this.

In the 1960s, Kathryn Kuhlman became "the most famous woman evangelist in the world."[46] Though she "captivated audiences" with "her electric personality, unique style of dress and speaking in a deliberate voice,"[47] she was reluctant to raise anyone up to carry her mantle.

After Kuhlman launched her foundation, it steadily grew. The organization "funded her radio and TV ministry and helped establish two dozen missions around the world."[48] Although the Kuhlman Foundation touched many lives, no succession plan was in place.

When pressed on this issue, Kuhlman said there's "no need to prepare a legacy." In 1975, Steve Strang, editor of *Charisma Magazine*, asked her "if she had designated a successor. She replied that Jesus would return before she died."[49]

Kuhlman was gravely mistaken. She passed away less than a year later from a heart condition. The woman evangelist was the lone voice for the ministry. No one else was positioned to carry on her mission.

Up to that time, the Kuhlman Foundation was a multi-million-dollar operation, facilitating mission projects, media broadcasts, and the circulation of publications. Along with other functions, they processed thousands of letters and became a lifeline to thousands of supporters.

Although the Foundation had key employees managing the business affairs, Kuhlman established no successor. To make matters worse, she "rewrote her will shortly before her death, leaving bequests to individuals rather than her own foundation."[50]

With a lack of funding and no recognized leader, the Kathryn Kuhlman Foundation was forced to pull back on missions and radio broadcasts. The once-vibrant organization ultimately ceased operations.

I could easily share a number of stories along these lines. A vast majority of ministries have no designated replacement. Aging leaders have selfishly made themselves the focus, jeopardizing the originating mandate. When it comes to mission, there's more at stake than a man or woman's legacy. Leaders need to see beyond themselves to a greater goal.

CHRIST FOR ALL NATIONS

It takes a unique person to start an organization or company. So it's no surprise that most ministry heads are Type-A personalities. They are take-charge kind of people and are notoriously reluctant to pass the baton.

One notable exception to this trend was Reinhard Bonnke. He launched a missions organization called Christ For All Nations. As Bonnke aged, he raised up a younger evangelist named Daniel Kolenda to work alongside him.

Bonnke treated Kolenda like a son and gave him the freedom to operate in his calling. Bonnke had Kolenda preach alongside him in overseas crusades and included the younger evangelist in the decision-making.

As Bonnke later grew ill and died, it was clear who was supposed to lead the organization: Kolenda. As a result, Christ For All Nations kept their momentum and did not lose contributors.

This organization never missed a step because the founder actively empowered the next generation. We can learn much from the wisdom of Reinhard Bonnke. Because of a fathering heart, his legacy will continue to expand for decades to come.

THE MEANING OF EMPOWERMENT?

What does empowerment mean? It's recognizing and cultivating what God's doing in someone else. Empowerment is identifying the callings of others and aiding them in their personal development. It's helping sons and daughters discover their destiny.

I'm not suggesting that a senior leader agrees to everything a younger leader wants. Emerging voices still need correction and redirection. But older figures should champion them as much as possible.

What if an established father harnessed and resourced the passions of his sons? This could be a catalyst for exponential growth in the organization.

Although difficult, leaders should empower others and help them discharge their giftings. When you're a seasoned leader on the front lines, you might not be comfortable with what others bring to the table. Their strengths may be in a wholly different area. But those with experience must remember that part of their mission is to enable the next generation to rise to greatness.

Validating and empowering others doesn't remove the distinctions or diminish the centrality of a senior leader. Not everyone in an organization is positioned to speak up about all matters. Roles vary, and some are truly positioned as final decision-makers.

People without the stature generally shouldn't make the rules. They need to learn to defer to the real fathers in the room. Recently I heard a business owner say it like this: "Too many cooks spoil the broth."

Understand that empowerment does not mean giving everything away but instead means positioning the next generation to arise and make meaningful contributions. Generosity is vital but so is wisdom and applied reason.

This will often result in tension. Although the next steps might be poorly defined, it's important to wrestle with this anyway. However, let me make this clear: If established leaders refuse to invest in those coming up, their support team will move on to someone who will. It would be tragic to lose our sons and daughters.

APPRENTICED TRAINING

A biblical standard of empowerment should have better acceptance in our circles. Some have characterized this technique as "apprenticed training." Throughout the New Testament, this pattern was repeatedly utilized.

Barnabas, the son of encouragement, furnished fatherly guidance to a newly redeemed Paul (Acts 13–14). Later, as Paul matured into his role as an apostle, he invested in Silas (Acts 16:19–40), Timothy (1 and 2 Timothy), Titus (Titus), and others.

In one of his last letters to Timothy, Paul encouraged his protégé to repeat this same pattern. The apostle wrote, "What you have heard from me in the presence of many witnesses entrust to faithful men who will be able to teach others also" (2 Timothy 2:2 NIV).

A crucial part of leadership is helping others activate their callings. A father unlocks wonderful realities for others when he helps his sons. Sometimes a leader's most remarkable achievement will be the individuals that he or she has raised up.

SOLOMON GENERATION

According to the pages of the Bible, David was the greatest king of Israel. By the Spirit of God and the sheer brute of his strength, he pushed out the technologically advanced Philistines and united the scattered tribes. He brought wealth and peace, re-establishing worship in Jerusalem. David demonstrated transformative leadership as few others did.

As the years progressed, David felt burdened to build a house for God. He envisioned a spectacular temple that would be the culmination of his reign. On a practical level, David was best positioned to do this. He could inspire and mobilize the people. This anointed king built a number of things from nothing.

Yet as David sought the Lord, he was informed that someone

else would accomplish his dream: Solomon, the son of David, the next generation who would be tasked with establishing God's house.

This revelation was likely tough for David. He probably looked at Solomon and thought, *My son has done nothing to deserve such a noble task*. Solomon hadn't fought wars or conquered giants. He was relatively ignorant and undisciplined, yet God still chose him to carry out this monumental work.

David, to his credit, deferred to God and empowered Solomon to implement his destiny. Though he knew his son wasn't ready for all the future held, David believed in him anyway. He acknowledged Solomon and honored him:

> David said, "My son Solomon is still young and inexperienced" . . . David ordered all the leaders of Israel to assist Solomon in this project. "The Lord your God is with you," he declared. (1 Chronicles 22:5, 17-18 NLT).

David was bold and brazen, but he was never positioned to accomplish everything. No one is strong enough for that. The highest goal for a father is to enable the next generation to step into their destiny. Legacies are measured long after a father is gone.

Years earlier, the Lord had revealed the following vision to David:

> You will have a son who will be a man of peace. I will give him peace with his enemies in all the surrounding lands. His name will be Solomon, and I will give peace and quiet to Israel during his reign. He is the one who will build a Temple to honor my name. He will be my son, and I will be his father. And I will secure the throne of his kingdom over Israel forever. (1 Chronicles 22:9-10 NLT)

Astounding events unfolded, just as the Lord decreed. Solomon built the house for the Lord. In later years, he declared, "Now the Lord my God has given me rest on every side; there is neither adversary nor evil occurrence" (1 Kings 5:4 NKJV). Solomon experienced blessings that his father never knew.

Ideally, our ceiling becomes the next generation's floor. The lesser draws upon all the advantages and wisdom that the greater provides. Our sons and daughters are positioned to carry our dreams and visions further than we're capable of doing.

Like David, we may not see the fulfillment of all that we hoped for. Some of what we've envisioned will take place through our sons and daughters. Whatever they accomplish will be part of your destiny.

6. LEADERS PROTECT

Transformative leaders *empower*, but they also *protect*. This is a crucial responsibility for organizational heads. Within every enterprise, someone must stop nefarious forces.

However, this responsibility is not usually applauded. In fact, most people will criticize this role. Protection is often misinterpreted by those who have a misconception of what it actually encompasses.

A neophyte might covet the creativity, decision-making, and accolades of a leadership position, but he or she doesn't see the accompanying friction points. A leader might seem harsh to outsiders when he or she takes a stand. The protection of an organization is often a thankless undertaking.

Frontline leaders are able to "provide a halo for the company when it faces threats."[51] They keep outside forces at bay. Sooner or later, opposing entities will attack and attempt to impede the vision. Few will side with an authority who tries to defend the cause. As a leader stands firm, some will outwardly oppose them.

In the business realm, detractors might sponsor constrictive laws or upend marketplaces. Less scrupulous competitors bribe city council members or write unfavorable reviews of products on Amazon. Although conflict can become bloodthirsty in the public square, a leader should embrace it.

Underneath it all, the battle is not against flesh and blood but against spiritual forces of darkness. (See Ephesians 6:10–18.) Leaders understand that they aren't fighting people but are combatting arguments, pretension, and ungodly obstacles. Rarely is it truly personal.

Those in authority will boldly stand against detractors. If attacked, they graciously hold the line. Mature leaders are willing to stand for what they believe in, even at a personal cost.

DENETHOR II, THE STEWARD OF GONDOR

In *The Return of the King,* the third movie adaption of J. R. R. Tolkien's *Lord of the Rings,* Mordor's treacherous hordes were advancing on the city of Minas Tirith. Evil forces were threatening to cut down all that was noble.

When Denethor II, the steward of the city, was warned, he did nothing to prepare for battle. He did not train his soldiers nor ignite the beacons for help.

Denethor was self-indulgent, eating and drinking gluttonously as the hordes of darkness advanced. One nobleman moaned, "The people of Gondor fell into ruin. The line of kings failed. The white tree withered. The rule of Gondor was given over to lesser men."[52]

Denethor, with his callous negligence, proved that he was no king. If the other warriors had not intervened, Denethor's passivity would have caused their destruction.

Honorable men are protectors of their land. They will leap into action when evil encroaches. Tolkien's story reminds us what leadership really means.

GENERAL WASHINGTON AND BENEDICT ARNOLD

During the American Revolution, alliances formed. Patriots from all walks of life joined together in colonial militias organized to respond to the oppressive taxation by the British monarchy.

As the skirmishes mounted, George Washington befriended Benedict Arnold, a pharmacist and bookseller. This entrepreneur's fortitude and resourcefulness swayed the general in his favor.

Tragically, Washington didn't recognize what was boiling under the surface. Arnold's drive was more for vainglory than for the Patriots' benefit. Soldiers alongside him thought he was selfish and divisive. In time, Arnold's pride would lead to a fall.

Overly ambitious, Arnold chastised his rivals and his commanding officers. In retribution, they withheld recognition, crediting others for his military achievements. Arnold was angered when the Continental Congress passed him over for promotions. The suggestion that his lessers outranked him was infuriating.

When George Washington stepped in and gave Arnold the command of West Point, a strategic military outpost, he didn't know that his friend was contemplating treachery.

Arnold loved living extravagantly and was deeply in debt. So the £20,000 that the British offered for the surrender of West Point was seductive. He became entrapped. To pay off debts and redress his sense of abandonment, Arnold agreed to turn against his friends.

Arnold's treasonous plan was exposed when Patriots discovered incriminating papers on a captured British officer. The soldiers took the evidence to Washington. The general struggled to accept the betrayal by his friend. Though bewildered, Washington knew that he could not delay. The destiny of the United States was on the line.

Washington dispatched armed forces to halt the plans. But before they could arrest the traitor, Arnold slipped away. The Patriots kept West Point from falling into the clutches of the British, but many felt that the noble cause had been tainted.

The fact that a major general from their own ranks would be a turncoat horrified the Continental Army. But no one was as perplexed as Washington. He had to live with the fact that a dear ally stabbed him in the back.

Wars are ruthless, and some of our friends might turn against us. But leaders are enduring and will do whatever is necessary to protect the community. They will fight to the end to ensure triumph.

PROTECTING PEOPLE FROM THEMSELVES

Leaders fight adversaries from without, but they also grapple with internal conflicts. Sometimes an overseer will have to confront the team, protecting individuals from themselves.

An entrepreneur named Tom was struggling with one of his employees, a man who helped him manage his business. His worker wasn't delivering the numbers and was rude to other employees.

Tom knew that his company had to be protected, but he also wanted to guide this failing manager. It would have been easier to fire the agitator, but short-term strategies might overlook the potential in others. Sometimes the harder way is best. This manager was a decent man. He just allowed some of his personal struggles to derail his job performance. In a sense, he needed to be protected from himself.

Tom brought this employee into his office. He looked at him and said, "Help me understand what's going on. You're living far below who God made you to be. What can we do to help you?" This heartfelt question opened up dialogue and helped turn the situation around.

As we were talking about what happened, Tom admitted that he hated these exchanges. The conversation could fill up the whole afternoon and infringe on his schedule. It would be fraught with emotion and awkward moments. Although Tom didn't enjoy it, he was willing to do what was necessary to protect his team.

Protection is a necessary part of leadership. Sometimes, a director might need to tell a trusted colleague no for the organization's greater good.

This principle shows up sometimes in segments of the sports world. I have heard of track coaches who removed runners from competitions because of excessive weight loss or eating disorders. Their concern for the athlete's health trumped their desire for a championship. Protection sometimes means losing a battle to win a war.

A leader fights to protect organizations and the people entrusted to their care. This is a vital responsibility for every enterprise. Sometimes the best offense is a good defense.

THE APOSTLE PAUL CONFRONTED EVIL

Now let's look at the church. Protection within a Christian fellowship often involves counteracting sin. Authentic leaders are prepared to confront wickedness at its roots, even when it's difficult.

The apostle Paul modeled this. He perceived that rampant immorality would undermine the faith of believers. So he was prepared to disfellowship a man who was in an unrepentant sexual relationship with his stepmother.

> I am told that a man in your church is living in sin with his stepmother. You are so proud of yourselves, but you should be mourning in sorrow and shame. And you should remove this man from your fellowship . . . You must call a meeting of the church. I will be present with you in spirit, and so will the power of our Lord Jesus. Then you must throw this man out and hand him over to Satan so that his sinful nature will be destroyed and he himself will

> be saved on the day the Lord returns. (1 Corinthians 5:1–2, 4–5 NLT)

Paul realized that if this congregation wasn't protected, several other issues would arise. Sin spreads through the ranks when it goes unchallenged. Leaders must readily defend the people and the honor of the Lord.

WEAKNESS OR WICKEDNESS

Leaders must have wisdom in all matters. In defending a ministry or another enterprise, we must differentiate between weakness and wickedness.

While *weakness* is characterized by foolishness, there is usually some semblance of decency underneath it all. The weak one may not be right, but they genuinely want to be.

Wickedness is fundamentally different. It's rooted in selfishness and deceit. These twisted individuals are more concerned with defending themselves than embracing what's right.

While *weakness* can generally be redirected, *wickedness* doesn't budge. It is unrelenting, like cancer circulating through the bloodstream.

There is grace for the weak but banishment for the wicked. Fundamentally, leaders can't even give an inch to treachery. Wretchedness must be cut off at the root. The longer cancer festers, the more the body suffers.

FOR THE SAKE OF THE PEOPLE

The need to offer protection is never a license to be overbearing and controlling. Leadership is strong but that exertion of power should be gentle, not oppressive. We aren't going for totalitarianism. A leader should exercise a selfless display of force, rooted in the greater good.

The Bible proclaims: "David realized that the LORD had confirmed him as king over Israel and had blessed his kingdom for the sake of his people Israel" (2 Samuel 5:12 NLT). David acquired authority solely for the benefit of the people. Power is for advancing the lives of the subjects, not for improving the status of the monarch.

This principle holds true today. Authority has nothing to do with a leader's fragile ego but is about helping people discover their full potential. The individuals in the community—not the one at the helm—exercise strength. Leaders defend the organization, not their own reputation.

Leaders need to regularly examine their hearts and ensure that their choices are rooted in the right motives. They must reflect on their actions and interactions. Effective leaders aren't self-serving; they stand for the greater good.

Protection is imperative. Leaders must stand guard against outside assaults as well as self-sabotage. Although leaders don't necessarily enjoy this part of governance, someone has to do it. Those who are prepared to employ their strength will help stave off ruin for the community.

7. LEADERS INSPIRE

Another crucial action point is *inspiration*. Governance should be strong but doesn't necessarily need to show an exertion of force. This is essential to grasp.

William was leading a 150-member congregation in the Midwest when his wife became ill. This disrupted his rhythm. This benevolent pastor could no longer manage the church as he was accustomed to.

To compensate, William leveraged his title. Barking orders, he appealed to his position as senior pastor. Rather than activating his subordinates and clarifying vision, William moved into command and control. In a moment of irritation, he told an associate, "I didn't hire you to think. I hired you to execute."

At first, his coercive approach worked. The people loved him and wanted to obey. But in time, problems developed. William was so preoccupied with what was going on at home that he didn't realize that he was dealing with management issues.

Many leaders don't know how to govern without leveraging their position. Most don't want to lead like the "rulers of the Gentiles" who "lord it over people" (Matthew 20:25). But for many authorities, it's the only model they know.

Multitudes are accustomed to leaders barking orders and making edicts. Strong, decisive rule has its place. It is not wrong but shouldn't be used excessively.

Jesus understood the pull of coercive power grabs and taught his leadership team the following:

> Those with great authority in this world rule oppressively over their subjects, like tyrants. But this is not your calling. You will lead by a completely different model. The greatest one among you will live as the one who is called to serve others. (Matthew 20:25-26 TPT)

In the end, transformational leaders don't control the dialogue or force issues. They work to empower others to make healthy choices. It's not that they couldn't wield their authority; it's just that they often choose not to.

DWIGHT D. EISENHOWER'S WISDOM

Before becoming president in 1953, Dwight D. Eisenhower had already gained international acclaim as Supreme Commander of the Allied Forces in World War II. He demonstrated leadership prowess in some of the most complex and difficult battles ever fought.

The charismatic and politically savvy Eisenhower spurred economic growth and provided strategic leadership in the early years of the Cold War. He persuaded Russia to make concessions in the Geneva Summit in 1955 and warned Americans about the dangers of the military-industrial complex.

This forward-thinking president recognized the opportunities and pitfalls of leadership as well as anyone in the mid-twentieth century. One of biggest takeaways we can learn from him was that governing by coercion doesn't work for the long-term. Effective leadership is always invitational. Eisenhower once said,

> By leadership, we mean the art of getting someone else to do something that you want done because he wants to do it, not because your position or power can compel him to do it, or your position of authority.[53]

Everyone would benefit from the wisdom of this military strategist and political force. Eisenhower's idea of governance was not the quickest or the easiest but produced results exponentially better over time.

Our influence goes much further when we help people discover for themselves what's right. Leadership, properly executed, is more about persuasion than control.

ON THE BASIS OF LOVE

Perhaps one of the clearest examples of aspirational leadership is found in the writings of the apostle Paul in the New Testament. He said, "Although in Christ I could be bold and order you to do what you ought to do, yet I prefer to appeal to you on the basis of love" (Philemon 1:8–9 NIV).

Paul acknowledges that he could exploit his rank and rule with force. Yet he doesn't go that route. Instead he persuades. Paul leads from love rather than position.

A leader could demand obedience—and may need to occasionally. But an organization is usually better served by encouragement and redirection. Fathering and sincere displays of love are the most effective means of persuasion.

Inspiration is an effective catalyst. It encourages honorable decision-making and activation. It calls the people to arise based on their identity and values. Paul and many of the early Christian leaders had insights that we need to return to.

MARTIN LUTHER KING, JR.

On August 28, 1963, Martin Luther King Jr., came before a quarter of a million people in Washington DC. Standing on the steps of the Lincoln Memorial, he shared his transformative vision for America. He cried out to those assembled, "I have a dream."

At the time of King's address, racial tensions were riding high. In the South, repressive laws made it difficult for Blacks to vote or receive an education. Individuals with darker skin were treated as second-class citizens.

It would have been sensible to damn the oppressors, which is what many did. The maligned certainly had the right to decry the sins against them. But King took a different approach. He chose to be aspirational:

> *I have a dream that one day on the red hills of Georgia, the sons of former slaves and the sons of former slave owners will be able to sit down together at the table of brotherhood.*
>
> *I have a dream that one day even the state of Mississippi, a state sweltering with the heat of injustice, sweltering with*

> *the heat of oppression, will be transformed into an oasis of freedom and justice.*
>
> *I have a dream that my four little children will one day live in a nation where they will not be judged by the color of their skin but by the content of their character. I have a dream today.*[54]

King appealed to the Declaration of Independence, the Emancipation Proclamation, and the innate longing for freedom in our nation. His plea was framed around a common decency that Americans believe about themselves. King called all American citizens to become who they already were.

King's speech was a pivotal moment that transformed the hearts of millions. But his words would not have had the same effect if they were coercive. Aspirational leadership touches hearts and changes the world.

THE STINGY CHURCH

I spoke with Jacob—a leader frustrated about the lack of generosity in his church. Contributions were down, and his payroll and insurance, along with his outreach efforts, were jeopardized.

This frustrated pastor scolded his congregation. "Shame on you for your stinginess and lack of concern. Jesus called us to be generous, and you're not fulfilling this role. You are burdened with everything but God. I'm almost ashamed to be your pastor."

Jacob assumed his congregation would feel shame and modify their behavior. Afterward, when the offering totals came in, he grew more irritated. Giving had diminished even more.

Jacob prepared to go back and hammer home his point again. But I persuaded him to embrace a different approach. I asked, "Is your goal increased giving or shame? You can have one or the other."

Jacob replied, "Obviously, I need to focus on receiving more contributions. But they're in the wrong, and I have the right to call them out."

I told this pastor that I understood his frustration. Yet rebuking the people might not get the outcome he was hoping for.

Many leaders are more concerned with defending their position than with bringing about necessary outcomes. The exposure of spiritual lethargy has its place. We need prophets and iconoclasts. But that is not the only way of confrontation.

I pointed out that leadership often works best if it's aspirational. Help people see who they could be and where God is taking them. Talk about the positive changes they can make, rather than their inaction. Speak to what they believe about themselves and draw upon it.

How we tell a story makes a difference. I once heard someone share the following observation: "No one ever sees themselves as the villain of the story. If you're recounting the story of David and his slingshot, no one will be thinking, 'I'm Goliath.'"

Telling someone that they're the villain is pointless because they'll never receive it. Instead, address them like a flawed hero—a decent person who has made mistakes. That's how most see themselves.

I told Jacob to pull instead of push. I pointed out that he should stand up with a big smile and a pervading sense of hope and then say something like the following:

> We're a generous congregation! God has called us to become this, and we're coming into this more every day. We step up and accomplish the purposes of God. We're learning to sacrifice and release what the Lord has blessed us with. So much needs to be done in the kingdom, and I'm so glad that God is empowering us to advance. Destiny is coming upon us, and we are about to witness some amazing things in this house.

I encouraged Jacob to boldly proclaim who they're becoming. Help them feel a sense of purpose. Let them understand that they can be even more, that they can go higher in Christ. Although hesitant, he told me he'd give it a shot.

When this pastor engaged his fellowship with hopeful rhetoric, the people responded enthusiastically. Jacob witnessed immediate changes. He finally understood that aspirational leadership worked better than the coercive approach that he had tried before.

HOW AUTHORITY IS EXPRESSED

Dynamics are changing around us. With unforeseen social, financial, and technological disruptions, individuals don't interact with leaders like they used to.

In previous eras, organizations tended to be centralized, regulated, and propelled by coercive authority. Power and position meant a great deal to people. But attitudes have changed.

Most no longer see a world as a hierarchal pyramid. In their experience, they no longer have limited information, resources, or skills available to them. So a leader who tries to leverage this to gain the upper hand won't be well-received. People are making it clear that they don't like to be talked down to.

Our emerging culture doesn't think in terms of hierarchy or even expertise. They take into perspective relationship, experience, and personal value. Years ago, people looked to the film critic Roger Ebert to determine whether a movie was worth watching. Now they ask their friends on social media.

Whether it's entertainment, advertisements, or politics, people don't respond as well to so-called experts. Coercive authority doesn't make sense to most. They listen more closely to those they are relationally aligned with.

I'm not minimizing the significance of positional roles. The Bible affirms legitimate power and hierarchal structures. As I previously mentioned, at times, leaders need to exert outward strength. Protection is a legitimate part of holding an organization together. But that approach should not be over-extended.

Inspirational leaders are not reluctant to leverage their authority, but they tend to do it indirectly. They don't abandon strength but merely reposition it.

Today, society needs individuals who inspire people to rise to their level of greatness. Rather than talking down, they're building up. Twenty-first-century America yearns for uplifting, aspirational leaders.

THE RIGHT TOOLS

While leadership is stimulating, it's also demanding. Overseers struggle to bear the burdens of an organization's maintenance and expansion. They never seem to have enough time to do it all.

I grabbed coffee with a young pastor named Blake. This thirty-two-year-old mentioned how difficult it was to hold his church together. He had to ensure that his facility was maintained, finances were coming in, and members were connected. He constantly wrote sermons and managed crises.

Blake told me, "I can never have a bad day. Everything in the organization is riding on me. It's overwhelming to have to always be on my mark."

I sympathized with Blake. Leadership is intense. On the one hand, it's beautiful; on the other, it's demanding. Responsibilities are multilayered and complex.

The person in charge can't just be competent in a few matters; they have to be proficient in many. An organizational leader, due to a limited budget and few volunteers, often has to be a jack-of-all-trades.

The apostle Paul highlighted some areas of responsibility to his protege, Timothy. He said, "Keep your head in all situations, endure hardship . . . discharge all the duties" (2 Timothy 4:5). This admonition applies to us as well.

It's exhilarating to learn that you're called to exert authority. You're graciously invited to take part in the increase of God's kingdom. But this responsibility is enormous. How could a frail man or woman carry out every task? No wonder Paul advised leaders that they should learn to endure hardship. He understood the problematic issues of leadership better than anyone.

MENTORS, MODELS, PARTNERS, AND FRIENDS

Every leader, no matter how gifted, will ultimately come up short. Even those with the most extraordinary abilities will not be able to accomplish everything alone—particularly with so many disruptions. Many challenges seem to lie before us.

Meg Wheatley, a popular leadership consultant, thinks that the way to advance in confusing seasons "is to attend to the quality of our relationships."[55] Too many on the front lines have allowed themselves to be isolated and disconnected. To move forward, leaders need to build better relationships. They must network, drawing from the strength and wisdom of others.

Leaders might commonly moan, "It's lonely at the top." But that sentiment is often tied to unsustainable older patterns. The Dead Sea in Israel is stagnant because no other water source flows into it. It doesn't matter what the manuals or entrenched voices argue; you weren't made to go it alone.

I told my pastor friend Blake that he would have to look outside himself for answers. A leader isn't called to do everything. Instead, they ensure everything gets done. Obviously, that's a whole different matter.

No one is supposed to be a one-man-band. Instead, they should think of themselves as a conductor in an orchestra. Leaders are conveners, enabling and being enabled to implement the mission.

Those at the helm need co-learners, co-laborers, and collaborators to assist with the work. Leaders benefit immensely when they draw from

- Mentors
- Models
- Partners
- Friends

Mentors are mature leaders who impart high-level wisdom and guidance. These individuals are further along in the journey and can help navigate uncharted waters. Those who have been where a leader is traveling can provide valuable insight.

It's satisfying to sit down with a *mentor*, but their understanding can be passed on indirectly through audio recordings or books. Emerging leaders need someone to teach them along the way.

Models flesh out needed outcomes. These personalities put theory into action. They embody the values. We all seek an example, and they provide this for us. We learn more easily from observation than from articulation. A great example is twice as valuable as well-intentioned advice.

A leader can find plenty of suitable models in books, but they're best found in relationship. Locate a transparent person whose life can be thoroughly examined. Never underestimate the relevance of demonstrated examples.

Partners hold up a leader's arms as Aaron and Hur did for Moses. (See Exodus 17:12.) The Old Testament lawgiver could not have carried out God's mission if it weren't for the contributions of these men. They kept Moses strong.

Partners work alongside a leader and do some of the following: resource, manage, and carry out urgent duties. They are irreplaceable supporters who uphold the mission of the institution.

Friends have the most to offer a besieged leader. They provide a kind word and loving support. These peers create a safe environment to talk. Friends are less focused on the organization than on the individual leading it. For them, it's not business, it's personal.

Jesus revealed in Scripture, "No one shows greater love than when he lays down his life for his friends" (John 15:13 ISV). Giving of yourself for others is the essence of friendship. Everyone needs a faithful confidant who stands with them through life's difficulties and trials.[56]

Never undervalue the contributions of others. Each of us receives extraordinary benefit from *mentors, models, partners,* and *friends*. These allies bring gifts to the table that we desperately need.

DIVINE FAVOR

As vital as it is to get help from others, the ultimate leadership catalyst comes from somewhere else—*divine favor*. When grappling with responsibilities, we must lean into the inexplicable wonder of grace. This wellspring is our source. Reflecting on this, the apostle Paul wrote,

> What I am now I am by the grace of God. The grace he gave me has not proved a barren gift. I have worked harder than any of the others—and yet it was not I but this same grace of God within me. (1 Corinthians 15:10-11 J. B. Phillips)

Contemporary leaders benefit from the wisdom, gifts, and competencies of others, but they will get nowhere without the Lord's favor. One will invariably make mistakes and come up short. A godly leader does all that he or she can but depends on God to make up what's lacking.

Because of extraordinary favor, I've accomplished things I should have never achieved. I've traveled across the United States, speaking to thousands. While doing this, I've developed relationships with authors and influential Christian leaders. Some of these figures have endorsed my books and taken time to interact with me face-to-face. Countless times, I've been seated in places that I don't belong.

A few years ago, I crowdfunded an astounding twenty thousand dollars to produce a three-volume hardback book series, *Regeneration: A Complete History of Healing in the Christian Church*[57] I was not prepared for what I encountered as I pulled together this complex project. It should have never worked, but it did—only because of God's grace.

Hundreds of times, divine favor has propelled me beyond what I could naturally expect. I've been encouraged by what Jesus said, "If you truly follow me as my disciple, the Father will shower his favor upon your life" (John 12:26 TPT).

Phenomenal leaders draw on something greater than themselves. Amber, my educator friend, said she prays every night for the wisdom and favor of God in her life. She doesn't wear her faith on her sleeve, but it shows in her daily engagements. Amber told me, "This truly is the secret of my success."

Great colleagues and fruitful execution are vital parts of leadership, but so is casting everything on Jesus. He's more than enough to carry you through. In him, you can endure hardship and discharge all the duties you have been entrusted to accomplish.

4

CONCLUSION

I talked with a non-profit director whose organization had lost momentum. After discussing methods and strategies, Chad said, “J. D., it feels like everything is flying off the rails. I’m not sure what we’re going to do.” I assured him that he wasn’t alone. All of us are toiling to keep our footing in a difficult season.

Trying times are bewildering. No one enjoys it when the rules change in the middle of the game. People feel agitated and powerlessness as life spins out of control.

It’s unnerving to lead in a disruptive era. Wisdom is sidelined in catastrophes. I’ve seen this repeatedly over the years.

Bedlam broke out in my college dorm decades ago. In defiance of leadership, guys lined the hall with mattresses. The long corridor was turned into a gauntlet as the students battled it out. One of my classmates said, “The inmates are running the asylum.” Inklings of truth are in every joke.

In 2020, I spoke with an entrepreneur who was wrestling with increased hostility from the government. A city council member demanded that he close his restaurant. If this owner didn’t pivot, everything that he built would be lost. The bureaucrat wasn’t sympathetic to his predicament. She said, "Maybe Congress will give you another bailout."

Multitudes are holding out for a hero amid the uncertainties. This outlook reminds me of the time when I spoke with a young girl decked in princess attire. She said, "Where's my knight in shining armor?" With a grin, I told her that she might have to wait for a while.

More recently, I discussed global conditions with a masked, socially distanced realtor. Tears welled up as she said, "Someone surely has answers. I'd hate to think that I have to do this all by myself." I assured her that she was not alone, and that a remarkable future was ahead.

Yearning for a hero isn't wrong. But that desire might be an impediment if heaven has different plans. What if you're commissioned to arise, called to be the hero in your own story?

Centuries ago, while under duress, the nation of Israel trekked through the desert. Their instincts led them to believe they'd find answers in another place. But God revealed that this wasn't the plan. Their solution was "not kept beyond the sea" in the hands of a distant hero. The Lord announced, "No, the message is very close at hand; it is on your lips and in your heart" (Deuteronomy 30:13–14 NLT).

In this crisis, Israel wasn't supposed to look outside their own community. The answer was ingrained in their voices. Rather than hunting for a pathfinder, they were to lead the way.

Many leaders lose their sense of direction, spurning their gifts and callings. When commissioned with a task, why look elsewhere? Those already in the driver's seat should just turn the key and start the engine.

A few years ago, I discussed the problem of disengagement with a friend. Cliff told me that leaders become too complacent and need to be shaken from time to time. He exclaimed, "You either change the world or the world changes you."[1]

So many leaders formulate and execute. They write strategies down but still come up short. Obstacles will invariably come up as we move into uncharted territories. Those without a map may stumble. But the tough keep getting up and finding new ways to advance.

THE BRIDGE TO NOWHERE

Sometimes the world changes so drastically that the ground moves out from under you. In these seasons, the finest education, tools, and strategies no longer help.

The citizens of Choluteca, Honduras, experienced this two decades ago. In the late 1990s, the Hazama Ando Corporation erected a steel bridge that could withstand gale force winds in this Latin American nation.

Not long after the bridge's completion, a Category 5 hurricane hit. As torrents of rain fell, Honduras was swamped. Although this edifice withstood the storms, its resilience hardly mattered. The Choluteca River had been re-routed in the deluge.

This hurricane changed the landscape and warped the course of the stream. The unbending steel edifice was now useless—a bridge to nowhere. Peter Muello, a journalist with the Associated Press, wrote,

> The graceful arches of the New Choluteca Bridge stand abandoned, a white concrete sculpture far from shore, linking nothing to nowhere. The Choluteca Bridge itself is perfect... except that it now straddles dry land. Mitch changed the course of the Choluteca River, and there is water where the access roads used to be.[2]

After disruptive changes, people look backward. They want to return to their previous stability. Hazama Ando, the corporation that constructed the bridge, researched ways to revert the river back to its old configuration.

Kinoshita Kenichi, a twenty-eight-year-old civil engineer, confessed, "It's very difficult to change the current." He said that everyone must accept that the Choluteca River is "in a totally different place."[3] Some things can't be reversed.

In this season, previous reliable practices no longer work. Now more than ever, we can't confuse the husk with the ear of corn. Medium and message are never the same. Don't fall in love with methods because they will invariably lose their effectiveness. The role of a leader is to reframe matters in terms of the irreducible core. Innovators can't afford to get lost in semantics.

A few of the leaders that I've spoken with during this last season are in denial. Some are in mourning or grappling with anger. It's unfair that the river changed so abruptly, but there's no going back. It's time to stop mourning old bridges that go nowhere.

A BETTER LEADERSHIP MODEL

Sometimes leaders are left with the unenviable job of sifting through the rubble. The future demands new configurations, but all is not lost. We can still hold on to what's good.

Truth isn't subjective, but applications must be relevant. Overextended claims turn social constructs on their head. The tribe must hear and understand the key points. Context truly matters.

About thirty years ago, an Assembly of God official met with a group of prospective ministers. He said, "Don't disqualify yourselves." Although this was sound guidance, Richard carried his idea to an extreme. He said,

> If you make a gaffe or have any shortcoming, the people will eat you alive. The masses want their leaders larger than life and without

> flaws. So, you better clean up your messes right now while there's still time. If not, you're finished.

I understood where Richard was coming from. Leadership is a high calling and must be marked by integrity. But he threatened the recruits with the following: "If you mess up, you may as well pack your bags and go home. Only those without flaws can lead."

High standards are nonnegotiable, but the reality of sonship and grace should trump impossible standards. Leadership is more than avoiding mistakes and maintaining a clean record.

Under Richard's program, the young ministers hid sins and evaded questions. Since leadership was a performance, they became Oscar-caliber actors. They knew that they couldn't let their guard down. One expressed it like this: "It was like living in a house without a restroom. We couldn't process pain or discharge toxins." This was a disaster waiting to happen.

Three of the ministers from that training are now divorced, and most don't serve in church. The outcome might have been different if we'd offered them a better model.

I've discovered that idealism can impede kingdom activation. Sometimes we think God is mad about what he finds only mildly irritating. Sin should never be minimized. Yet Jesus sees our weaknesses and still extends his hand. Christian leaders can commonly create rigid mechanisms. But our governance should mirror heaven more than our own proclivities.

In this changing age, leadership will look different than we imagined. Sometimes God intentionally breaks paradigms. We must see what's happening as situations often differ from how they appear. Not all of our bridges still serve a purpose.

BEAUTY FOR ASHES

I'm friends with a man who once lost his way. During mid-life, Sid became ensnared in an addiction. This shattered father not only lost his job but also his family. For him, the future dimmed. But with God's mercy and grace, circumstances changed.

After repenting and fleeing alcohol's grip, Sid started a construction business. As the company grew, he began hiring ex-convicts. My friend provided guidance and treated them with compassion, helping turn their lives around. Several encountered Jesus and gained meaning in life.

Although his life had fallen apart, my friend turned to God and found that he still had a purpose. Because of his earlier missteps, most considered Sid a failure, but they were wrong.

From splintered fragments, God brings restoration. The Bible verse my friend liked to share proclaimed, "To all who mourn in Israel, he will give a crown of beauty for ashes, a joyous blessing instead of mourning" (Isaiah 61:3 NLT).

Sid told his employees, "We often build a promising future on the pain of the past." His inspiring story reminds us that leadership can arise from our worst disasters. God enjoys shattering assumptions. Sometimes heaven's answers break our little boxes.

As I witnessed what Sid accomplished, I realized Richard, the official from the early 90s, underestimated the power of grace. Damaged individuals can sometimes lead. While authority is rooted in identity and action, it also radiates from the unfathomable love of God.

The Lord breathes on whatever (and whoever) he wants. Sometimes, he will bless matters and people outside our frame of reference. We might need to reframe our idea of how the world operates. Our well-thought-out practices are not necessarily wrong; they're just incomplete.

Seasons of disruption often reveal that our vision is too small. A crisis can be a pathway to a whole new realm of engagement.

THE SHIFT

We live in an era where life seems to race a million miles an hour. Deadly health crises and disturbances unfold. Businesses are failing, and myriads are losing their footing. Amid the chaos, the road ahead has become cloudy.

Many are crying out for mothers and fathers. They're tired of the restlessness and pain. A common refrain is "Surely someone with wisdom and courage can help me." Society needs a captain to aid them as they navigate the turbulent seas.

Beneath the turmoil, God is at work. Though we might not see it, he's restoring beauty and wonder. In this age, he is releasing grace like never before. Many men and women are rising above the fray and discovering their destinies. Leaning into this moment, leaders are asking questions, making connections, and seizing opportunities.

A glorious future is unfolding. Mercy and grace are on display. Gifted sons and daughters are commissioned to reflect God, accomplish exploits, and revolutionize the world.

God is asking each of us to take a second look at what he's doing. In a topsy-turvy world, he's unleashing creators, educators, ministers, and entrepreneurs. All of us are a vital part of heaven's advance.

How thrilling to be on the cusp of this earth-shattering shift.

NOTES

INTRODUCTION

1. For centuries, culture reinvented itself every generation. But what used to transpire every forty years now occurs every eighteen months. The speed of cultural change is now more than ten times what it was a decade ago. See Doug Paul, *Ready or Not: Kingdom Innovation for Brave New World* (100 Movements Publishing, 2020).
2. George Galloway quoted in Scott Galloway, P*ost Corona: From Crisis to Opportunity* (New York: Portfolio, 2020), xvi.
3. Marshall McLuhan, *Understanding Media: The Extensions of Man* (Cambridge, MA: MIT Press, 1994), x.
4. Shane Hipps, *Flickering Pixels* (Grand Rapids, Michigan: Zondervan, 2009), 47.
5. Cara Giaimo, "The Spiky Blob Seen Around the World, " *New York Times* (April 1, 2020).
6. Fareed Zakaria, *Ten Lessons for a Post-Pandemic World* (New York: W. W. Norton & Company, 2020), 3.
7. Scott Galloway, P*ost Corona: From Crisis to Opportunity* (New York: Portfolio, 2020), xvi-xvii
8. Ibid., xviii.
9. Ibid., 84.
10. See Tim Arango, Nicholas Bogel-Burroughs, Derrick Bryson Taylor, Audra D. S. Burch, Maria Cramer, John Eligon, Manny Fernandez, Christine Hauser, Neil MacFarquhar, Kwame Opam, Lucy Tompkins and Neil Vigdor, "What We Know About the Death of George Floyd in Minneapolis," *The New York Times* (Feb. 15, 2021).
11. The phrase, "The Revolution Will Not Be Televised" was originally a slogan of the Black Power movement of the 1960s. Gil Scott-Heron. Gil Scott-Heron, "The Revolution Will Not Be televised," Pieces of a Man (Flying Dutchman, 1971)
12. Talia Lavin, "How 'Eat the Rich' Became the Rallying Cry for the Digital Generation," *GQ* (November 5, 2020).
13. Elle Hunt, "What does it mean to be a 'Karen'? Karens explain," *Guardian* (May 13, 2020).
14. Ben Zimmer, "'OK Boomer': A Defining Generation Becomes a Label for Irrelevance," *Wall Street Journal* (December 21, 2019).
15. Jean-Jacques Rousseau quoted in Talia Lavin, "How 'Eat the Rich' Became the Rallying Cry for the Digital Generation," GQ (November 5, 2020).
16. Philip Rucker and Robert Costa, "Election reveals deeper divides between red and blue America," *Wall Street Journal* (November 4, 2020).

17. See Nelson D. Schwartz, Ben Casselman, and Ella Koeze, "How High Is Unemployment? Literally Off the Charts," *The New York Times* (May 8, 2020).
18. Tony Morgan, "Welcome to Multisite Church in the New Normal" *Unstuck Group* (November 2020).
19. Phillip Inman, "Pandemic is Chance to Reset Global Economy, Says Prince Charles," *The Guardian* (June 3, 2020).
20. Jerry Lee Lewis, "A Whole Lotta Shakin' Goin' On," *Sun Records* (April 15, 1957).
21. Editors, "Black Death," *History* (July 6, 2020).
22. Fareed Zakaria, *Ten Lessons for a Post-Pandemic World* (New York: W. W. Norton & Company, 2020), 6.
23. Ibid., 97-98.
24. Abraham Lincoln, *First Inaugural Address* (speech, Washington, DC, March 4, 1861). http://www.abrahamlincolnonline.org/lincoln/speeches/1inaug.htm (accessed November 28, 2020).
25. T. S. Eliot, "Little Gidding," *Four Quartets* (London: Harcourt, 1943), st. v, lines 28-29. http://www.columbia.edu/itc/history/winter/w3206/edit/tseliotlittlegidding.html (accessed November 29, 2020).

1. LEADING WITH A WEAK HAND

1. See Annie Lowry, "Readers Without Borders: What killed the big-box retailer? Hint: It wasn't the Internet," *Slate* (July 20, 2011).
2. Julian Ryall, "Toyota overtakes GM as world's largest car manufacturer," *The Telegraph* (January 22, 2009).
3. Bill Vlasic, "G.M. Vow to Slim Includes Top Ranks," *New York Times* (July 10, 2009).
4. Ibid.
5. Scott Galloway, *Post Corona: From Crisis to Opportunity* (New York: Portfolio, 2020), 4.
6. General Motors television commercial. There's nothing as American as "baseball, hot dogs, apple pie, and Chevrolet." (1974).
7. Scott D. Anthony, "Kodak's Downfall Wasn't About Technology," *Harvard Business Review* (July 15, 2016).
8. Fareed Zakaria, *Ten Lessons for a Post-Pandemic World* (New York: W. W. Norton & Company, 2020), 99.
9. See Ibid., 125.
10. "Amazon was up 67%, and JCPenney was bankrupt." Scott Galloway, *Post Corona: From Crisis to Opportunity* (New York: Portfolio, 2020), 4.
11. Ibid.
12. Editor, "The Outsiders," *The Economist* (May 24, 2012).
13. Claire Atkinson, "Why have more than 1,300 CEOs left their post in the past year?" *NBC News* (November 6, 2019).
14. Fareed Zakaria, *Ten Lessons for a Post-Pandemic World* (New York: W. W. Norton & Company, 2020), 100.

15. Mark Greenbaum, "Lincoln's Do-Nothing Generals," *New York Times* (November 27, 2011).
16. Ibid.
17. See Rick Peristein, "Watergate Scandal," *Britanica* (September 10, 2010).
18. Stephen Hess, "Jimmy Carter: Why He Failed," *Brookings Institute* (June 1978).
19. Ronald Reagan, "The Living Room Candidate," Television Commercial, 1980.
20. See "How Bad Will It Get? Will the Wuhan Virus become a Pandemic?" *The Economist Magazine* (February 1, 2020).
21. Alasdair Sandford, "Coronavirus: Half of Humanity Now on Lockdown as 90 Countries Call for Confinement," *Euronews* (April 3, 2020).
22. See Benjamin Siegel, Soo Rin Kim, and Katherine Faulders, "Local officials frustrated as governors change rhetoric and send mixed messages on coronavirus," *ABC News* (June 30, 2020).
23. Fareed Zakaria, *Ten Lessons for a Post-Pandemic World* (New York: W. W. Norton & Company, 2020), 46-47.
24. Ibid., 153.
25. See J. D. King, *Why You've Been Duped Into Believing that the World is Getting Worse* (Lees Summit, Missouri: Christos, 2019).
26. Tom Rainer, *The Post-Quarantine Church: Six Urgent Challenges and Opportunities That Will Determine the Future of Your Congregation* (Carol Stream, Illinois: Tyndale, 2020), 110.
27. See "Cottonwood Christian Center v. City of Cypress," Becket Fund for Religious Liberty (2015).
28. R. G. Robins, *Pentecostalism in America* (Santa Barbara, California: Praeger, 2010), 132–133.
29. Tom Rainer, *The Post-Quarantine Church: Six Urgent Challenges and Opportunities That Will Determine the Future of Your Congregation* (Carol Stream, Illinois: Tyndale, 2020), 41, 51.
30. Andy McAdams, "The Condition of the Church in America," *Monday Morning Insights* (December 2005).
31. Rainer's research quoted in "7 Startling Facts: An Up Close Look at Church Attendance in America," *Outreach Magazine* (April 10, 2018).
32. Darren Rogers, "Assemblies of God 2015 Statistics Released, Growth Spurred by Ethnic Transformation," *Flower Pentecostal Heritage Center* (June 24, 2016).
33. Kate Shellnutt, "Southern Baptists See Biggest Drop in 100 Years," *Christianity Today* (June 3, 2020).
34. Lorenzo Lebrija, "Looking Ahead," in *We Shall Be Changed: Questions For the Post-Pandemic Church*, ed. Mark D. W. Edington (New York: Church Publishing, 2020), 13-18. Lebrija draws data from Sandra L. Colby and Jennifer M. Ortman, "Projections of the Size and Composition of the U.S. Population: 2014 to 2060," *U.S. Census Bureau* (March 2015).
35. Tod Bolsinger, *Canoeing the Mountains* (Downer's Grove, Illinois: Intervaristy Press, 2018), 16.
36. See George Barna, *What Americans Believe* (Ventura, California: Regal Books, 1991).

37. Richard J. Krejcir, Ph.D., "Statistics on Pastors," *Francis A. Schaeffer Institute of Church Leadership Development* (1992, 2004, 2007). Interestingly, Krejcir found that only 32% of church leaders felt the ability to bring about change in the church was important. Only 26% of pastors felt that the ability to teach the Bible effectively was important. Only 19% felt the ability to model authentic faith and character was important. These figures are even more disturbing.
38. Craig Welch, "The rise and fall of Mars Hill Church," *Seattle Times* (September 13, 2014).
39. Mark Driscoll quoted in ibid. Driscoll also described the United States as a "pussified nation" of "homoerotic worship loving momma's boy sensitive emasculated neutered" men raised by "burned feministed single mothers."
40. Ben Tertin, "The Painful Lessons of Mars Hill: What can we learn from the collapse of Mark Driscoll's church?" *Christianity Today* (December 16, 2014).
41. Some felt that Driscoll and Mars Hill's ambitions were a byproduct of Seattle's culture. "Some say, 'Let's deliver packages,' but Seattle says, 'No. Let's make it *Amazon*.' Some say, 'Let's have coffee,' but Seattle says, 'No. Let's make it *Starbucks*.' 'Let's have a grocery store.' 'No! Let's make it *Costco*.' *Microsoft*. *Google*. *Boeing*. Seattle is about power, expansion, and world domination." Ben Tertin, "The Painful Lessons of Mars Hill: What can we learn from the collapse of Mark Driscoll's church?" *Christianity Today* (December 16, 2014).
42. Mars Hill member quoted in Joy Tibbs, "The rise and fall of Mark Driscoll," *Premier Christianity* (December 2014).
43. Ben Tertin, "The Painful Lessons of Mars Hill: What can we learn from the collapse of Mark Driscoll's church?" *Christianity Today* (December 16, 2014).
44. Mark Driscoll quoted in Joy Tibbs, "The rise and fall of Mark Driscoll," *Premier Christianity* (December 2014).
45. Tod E. Bolsinger, *Canoeing the Mountains: Christian Leadership in Uncharted Territory* (Downer's Grove, Illinois: InterVarsity Press, 2018), 16.
46. Ibid., 17-18.
47. Kevin Graham Ford quoted in ibid., 18.
48. For further details on this, see J.D. King, *Why You've Been Duped into Believing that the World is Getting Worse* (Lee's Summit, Missouri: Christos Publishing, 2019).
49. Only 795 out of 3,143 U.S. counties reported increases. *See* "In U.S., Decline of Christianity Continues at Rapid Pace," *Pew Research Center* (October 17, 2019).
50. See David Olsen, *The American Church in Crisis: Groundbreaking Research based on a National Database of over 200,000 Churches* (Grand Rapids, Michigan: Zondervan, 2008). Another study in *The Journal for the Scientific Study of Religion* by sociologists C. Kirk Hadaway and Penny Long Marler backs up Olsen's findings. Their report reveals the number of people worshipping each week is 52 million, instead of 132 million. C. Kirk Hadaway and Penny Long Marler "How Many Americans Attend Worship Each Week? An Alternative Approach to Measurement" *The Journal for the Scientific Study of Religion* (August 2005).
51. Jeffrey M. Jone, "U.S. Church Membership Down Sharply in Past Two Decades," *Gallup* (April 18, 2019).

52. Carey Nieuwhof, "7 Ways to Respond As People Attend Church Less Often," *CareyNieuwhof.com* (July 2013). (accessed December 18, 2020).
53. Thom Rainer, "How COVID-19 has Changed Revitalization," *Facebook* (November 14, 2020).
54. Andy McAdams, "The Condition of the Church in America," *Monday Morning Insights* (December 2005).
55. Elise Erikson Barrett, "Working Together as the Way" in *We Shall Be Changed: Questions For the Post-Pandemic Church,* ed. Mark D. W. Edington (New York: Church Publishing, 2020), 42.
56. Some of the local congregations have "good reason to fear that they may not survive this time." Elise Erikson Barrett, "Working Together as the Way" in *We Shall Be Changed: Questions For the Post-Pandemic Church,* ed. Mark D. W. Edington (New York: Church Publishing, 2020), 41.
57. Pat Dooris, "Rioters damage church, shops in downtown Portland," *KGW8* (November 5, 2020).

2. THE TENSION OF BEING AND DOING

1. *Chariots of Fire,* written by Colin Welland (Warner Brothers, 1981).
2. Eric Liddell quoted in "Eric Liddell is more famous for the race he did not run than the one he did," *The Daily Dose* (September 18, 2018).
3. Mother Teresa quoted in Kathryn Spink *Mother Teresa: A Complete Authorized Biography* (New York: HarperCollins, 1997), 37.
4. The Norwegian Nobel Committee, "The Nobel Peace Prize" (1979).
5. Michael Jordan, Bio, *National Basketball Association,* www.nba.com (accessed September 2, 2006).
6. Harry Truman quoted in "'The Buck Stops Here' Desk sign," *Truman Library,* https://www.trumanlibrary.gov/education/trivia/buck-stops-here-sign (Accessed November 15, 2020).
7. Ibid.
8. Winston Churchill delivered this speech to the House of Commons of the United Kingdom on June 18, 1940. This speech was referenced in *The War Illustrated* (June 28, 1940), 686-687.
9. Winston Churchill, "The Price of Greatness," *Harvard University* (September 6, 1943). https://winstonchurchill.org/resources/speeches/1941-1945-war-leader/the-price-of-greatness-is-responsibility/ (accessed November 18, 2020).
10. See N. R. Kleinfield, "Tylenol's Rapid Comeback," *The New York Times* (September 17, 1983).
11. Tod E. Blosinger, *Leadership for a Time of Pandemic: Practicing Resilience* (Downer's Grove, Illinois: Intervarsity Press, 2020), 12.

3. LEADERSHIP MECHANICS

1. Tod Bolsinger, *Canoeing the Mountains* (Downer's Grove, Illinois: Intervaristy Press, 2018), 21.
2. Ibid., 14.
3. Ben Beaumont-Thomas, "Vinyl records outsell CDs in US for first time since 1980s," *The Guardian* (September 14, 2020).
4. T. S. Elliot, "The Hollow Men," in *Poems: 1909–1925* (London: Harcourt, Brace and World, 1925, 1963).
5. Teddy Roosevelt quoted in Suzy Platt, *Respectfully Quoted: A Dictionary of Quotations* (New York: Barnes & Noble, 1993), 123.
6. "TR and the Panama Canal," *The American Experience* (Public Broadcasting System, 2020).
7. Lillian Cunningham, "How Teddy Roosevelt created the modern American presidency," *The Washington Post* (June 27, 2016).
8. John Maxwell quoted in Scott Buchanan, "Ready to Answer the Call," *The Ohio Beacon* (May 14, 2020).
9. "Uber transformed a physical industry—taxicabs—into one whose essence was an information network, created and maintained by software." Fareed Zakaria, *Ten Lessons for a Post-Pandemic World* (New York: W. W. Norton & Company, 2020), 100.
10. Seth Fiegerman, "Uber's first investors open up about their wild ride," *CNN Business* (May 10, 2019).
11. See Brandon Showalter, "ALS Ice Bucket Challenge co-creator dies 7 years after diagnosis," *The Christian Post* (November 24, 2020).
12. Katie Rogers, "The 'Ice Bucket Challenge' Helped Scientists Discover a New Gene Tied to A.L.S.," *New York Times* (July 27, 2016).
13. James Murphy, "Avoidance Is No Longer an Option," in *We Shall Be Changed: Questions For the Post-Pandemic Church*, ed. Mark D. W. Edington (New York: Church Publishing, 2020), 53-56.
14. See Mark Deymaz, with Harry Li, *The Coming Revolution in Church Economics: Why Tithes and Offerings Are No Longer Enough, and What You Can Do About It* (Grand Rapids, Michigan, 2019).
15. Adam Grant, *Originals: How Non-conformists Move the World* (New York: Viking, 2016), 41.
16. Doug Paul, *Ready Or Not: Kingdom Innovation for a Brave New World* (100 Movements Publishing, 2020), 25.
17. See Howard A. Snyder, *The Radical Wesley: The Patterns and Practices of a Movement Maker* (Franklin, TN: Seedbed, 2014).
18. Grace Dean, "Americans are spending more on vinyl records than cds for the first time since the 1980s," *Business Insider* (September 14, 2020).
19. Fareed Zakaria, *Ten Lessons for a Post-Pandemic World* (New York: W. W. Norton & Company, 2020), 104.
20. Scott Galloway, *Post Corona: From Crisis to Opportunity* (New York: Portfolio, 2020), 19.

21. Ibid., 16.
22. Fareed Zakaria, *Ten Lessons for a Post-Pandemic World* (New York: W. W. Norton & Company, 2020), 184.
23. Jeffrey D. Lee, "Paschal Leaders for a Paschal Church," in *We Shall Be Changed: Questions For the Post-Pandemic Church*, ed. Mark D. W. Edington (New York: Church Publishing, 2020), 67-70.
24. "The rising generation has grown up on screens, and is comfortable with online interactions to a degree my generation cannot comprehend." Scott Galloway, *Post Corona: From Crisis to Opportunity* (New York: Portfolio, 2020), 144.
25. Doug Paul, *Ready or Not: Kingdom Innovation for Brave New World* (100 Movements Publishing, 2020), 108.
26. Tom Rainer, *The Post-Quarantine Church: Six Urgent Challenges and Opportunities That Will Determine the Future of Your Congregation* (Carol Stream, Illinois: Tyndale, 2020), 26.
27. Ibid., 28-29.
28. Will Mancini and Cory Hartman, *Future Church: Seven Laws of Real Church Growth* (Grand Rapids, Michigan: Baker Publishing Group, 2020), 17.
29. Susan, a formerly active church attender, writing in a Facebook post directed to Tom Rainer, *The Post-Quarantine Church: Six Urgent Challenges and Opportunities That Will Determine the Future of Your Congregation* (Carol Stream, Illinois: Tyndale, 2020), 95.
30. Galloway writes, "a generation that comes of age in the pandemic may not perceive the same value in the proximity my generation cherished." Scott Galloway, *Post Corona: From Crisis to Opportunity* (New York: Portfolio, 2020), 148.
31. Carey Nieuwhof "Guest Column: Carey Nieuwhof on Generational Preferences for In-Person Worship Post-COVID," *Barna Group* (November 11, 2020).
32. Will the church "have a missiology audacious enough to share the gospel in an age starkly characterized by the computer-integrated buffered self?" C. Andrew Doyle, "Everything Has Changed? Leadership for the New Mission Age " in *We Shall Be Changed. Questions For the Post-Pandemic Church*, ed. Mark D. W. Edington (New York: Church Publishing, 2020), 75-80.
33. Doug Paul, *Ready Or Not: Kingdom Innovation for a Brave New World* (100 Movements Publishing, 2020), 18.
34. See Ed Stetzer, "Church Planter's Challenge: Leadership Development and Reproducing Culture," *Catalyst* (February 2011).
35. Doug Paul, *Ready or Not: Kingdom Innovation for Brave New World* (100 Movements Publishing, 2020), 125.
36. Laura Sydell, "Has Apple Lost Its Innovation Mojo?" *NPR* (April 10, 2017).
37. *Think Different* is an Apple advertising campaign thought to be a response to IBM's slogan "Think."
38. Ibid.
39. Steve Jobs quoted in Dave Smith, "What everyone gets wrong about this famous Steve Jobs quote, according to Lyft's design boss," *Business Insider* (April 19, 2019).
40. Ibid.

41. Steve Jobs, Commencement Speech, Stanford University (June 12, 2005). https://news.stanford.edu/2005/06/14/jobs-061505/ (accessed October 20, 2020).
42. Laura Sydell, "Has Apple Lost Its Innovation Mojo?" *NPR* (April 10, 2017).
43. "What we want from Apple is something that makes us emotional, even unconsciously—say, truly beautiful and sophisticated design that we can't resist. Beefing up functional value, like expanding camera features, isn't attractive because everyone else is doing the exact same thing." Atsushi Osanai, a professor at *Waseda University* in Tokyo, quoted in Peter Cohan, "3 Signs That Apple Has Lost Its Innovation Mojo," *Forbes* (January 14, 2019).
44. Bob Burrough quoted in ibid.
45. Scott Galloway, *Post Corona: From Crisis to Opportunity* (New York: Portfolio, 2020), 187.
46. Peter Smith, "Forty years after death, Kathryn Kuhlman still inspires a small but steady flock," *Pittsburgh Post-Gazette* (February 13, 2016).
47. Ibid.
48. Editor, "Kathryn Kuhlman's Foundation Shutters Doors Forty Years After Her Death," *Charisma* (February 19, 2016).
49. Peter Smith, "Forty years after death, Kathryn Kuhlman still inspires a small but steady flock," *Pittsburgh Post-Gazette* (February 13, 2016).
50. Ibid.
51. Scott Galloway, *Post Corona: From Crisis to Opportunity* (New York: Portfolio, 2020), 93.
52. Peter Jackson, Philippa Boyens, and Fran Walsh, *The Lord of the Rings: The Return of the King* script (New Line Cinema, 2003).
53. President Dwight D. Eisenhower, "Remarks at the Annual Conference of the Society for Personnel Administration," (May 12, 1954). https://www.presidency.ucsb.edu/documents/remarks-the-annual-conference-the-society-for-personnel-administration (accessed December 17, 2020).
54. Martin Luther King, Jr., "I Have a Dream," *March on Washington for Jobs and Freedom* (August 28, 1963). https://kinginstitute.stanford.edu/king-papers/documents/i-have-dream-address-delivered-march-washington-jobs-and-freedom (accessed December 14, 2020).
55. Margaret J. Wheatley, "When Change Is Out of Our Control," in *Human Resources for the 21st Century*, Marc Effron, Robert Gandossy, and Marshall Goldsmith, eds. (Hoboken, New Jersey: Wiley, 2003), 187-194.
56. It would take me considerable time to discuss all the people who have befriended and encircled me. I wouldn't have gone very far without the support of these people. I am blessed beyond measure.
57. See J.D. King, *Regeneration: A Complete History of Healing in the Christian Church, three volumes* (Lee's Summit, Missouri: Christos Publishing, 2017). This book series is available on *Amazon* or at www.theresurgencestore.com.

4. CONCLUSION

1. Missionary Cliff Pash (1951-2018). Consider supporting *Advancing the Kingdom Ministries*, his ongoing mission in Uganda. https://www.atkinternational.com *Advancing the Kingdom*, 1935 Alabama St., Lawrence, KS, 66046-2647.
2. Peter Muello, "Bridge Damage Hampers Mitch Relief," *Associated Press* (November 16, 1998).
3. Kinoshita Kenichi quoted in ibid.

About J.D. King

J.D. King is an author, speaker, publisher, and leadership coach. In addition to consulting, developing training resources, and writing books, King has composed blog posts garnishing over 1.5 million page views.

King consults, equips leaders and is an associate pastor at World Revival Church in Kansas City, Missouri.

To find out more about J.D. and how he could speak to your group, visit him online:

Email: jdking@wrckc.com
Blog: jdking.net
Twitter: @jdkinginsights
Facebook: authorjdking
Bookstore: TheResurgenceStore.com

Also Available From Christos Publishing:

Why You've Been Duped Into Believing That The World Is Getting Worse

"For us Baby Boomer Christians who grew up on The Late Great Planet Earth, the future was deliciously and fascinatingly evil. J.D. King, in his latest book, asserts that we have been "duped" by this gloomy view of the future. Via numerous documented metrics, King shows that the influence of Christian values—and the growth of Christianity itself—is raising the quality of life around the globe."

—**JON MARK RUTHVEN, PhD.**
Author of *On the Cessation of the Charismata* and *What's Wrong with Protestant Theology*

Find out more at TheResurgenceStore.com

Christos Publishing

REGENERATION

A Complete History of Healing in the Christian Church

"Probably the most extensive treatment of healing in church history available."
- Craig Keener, Ph.D.

"This will surely become a foundational resource for anyone studying healing in the future."
– Pneuma Journal

Find out more at *TheResurgenceStore.com*

Christos Publishing

Also Available From Christos Publishing:

Faith Healing

Insights From Ethan Otis Allen, The First American Healing Evangelist

A quarter of a century before Smith Wigglesworth, John G. Lake, and Maria Woodworth-Etter, Ethan Otis Allen pioneered an extraordinary move of God. Rising from abject poverty, this uneducated man became, in the words of A.B. Simpson, "Father of divine healing in America."

Who was this forgotten man and what did he discover about the mysteries of the Kingdom of God?

Find out more at TheResurgenceStore.com

Christos Publishing

Also Available From Christos Publishing:

Healing in History Series

The Healing in History Series by J.D. King is a multi-volume collection that explores the works of God through numerous Christian traditions. Be amazed at the wonderful stories of healing in multiple Christian traditions.

Find out more at TheResurgenceStore.com

Christos Publishing

Also Available From Christos Publishing:

He Sent His Word And Healed Them:

Every Healing Scripture

This book—241 scriptures in bold readable type—was compiled to encourage reflection, prayer, and biblical confession.

In the midst of unspeakable affliction, God sent His word and released healing.

Find out more at TheResurgenceStore.com

Christos Publishing